# THE POWER OF THE PAUSE
## *The Wonder of Our Here & Now*

# WISING UP ANTHOLOGIES

ILLNESS & GRACE : TERROR & TRANSFORMATION

FAMILIES: *The Frontline of Pluralism*

LOVE AFTER 70

DOUBLE LIVES, REINVENTION &
THOSE WE LEAVE BEHIND

VIEW FROM THE BED: VIEW FROM THE BEDSIDE

SHIFTING BALANCE SHEETS:
*Women's Stories of Naturalized Citizenship & Cultural Attachment*

COMPLEX ALLEGIANCES:
*Constellations of Immigration, Citizenship, & Belonging*

DARING TO REPAIR: *What Is It, Who Does It & Why?*

CONNECTED: *What Remains As We All Change*

CREATIVITY & CONSTRAINT

SIBLINGS: *Our First Macrocosm*

THE KINDNESS OF STRANGERS

SURPRISED BY JOY

CROSSING CLASS: *The Invisible Wall*

RE-CREATING OUR COMMON CHORD

GOODNESS

FLIP SIDES
*Truth, Fair Play & Other Myths We Choose to Live By:
Spot Cleaning Our Dirty Laundry*

ADULT CHILDREN:
*Being One, Having One & What Goes In-Between*

# THE POWER OF THE PAUSE
## The Wonder of Our Here & Now

*Heather Tosteson & Charles D. Brockett*
Editors

Wising Up Press

Wising Up Press
P.O. Box 2122
Decatur, GA 30031-2122
www.universaltable.org

Copyright © 2022 by Wising Up Press

*All rights reserved. No part of this book may be used or reproduced in any manner whatsoever without written permission, except in the case of brief quotations embodied in critical articles or reviews.*

Catalogue-in-Publication data is on file with the Library of Congress.
LCCN: 2022943788

Wising Up ISBN: 978-1-7376940-4-5

To those who saw us through,
to those we lost,
for hidden gifts that lifted us,
for gracious grounding . . .

# CONTENTS

**HEATHER TOSTESON**
*The Power of the Pause: The Wonder of Our Here & Now* — 1

## I. MEDITATION

**KATHIE GIORGIO**
*Sitting* — 8

**DIANE ELAYNE DEES**
*The Space Within* — 16
*Sacred Circle* — 17
*Taste* — 18

**NADEL HENVILLE**
*Catholicism + ADHD* — 19

**JAMES WYSHYNSKI**
*Meditation with Two Voices* — 24
*Morning Commute, 9:17 A.M.* — 26

**LARRY LEFKOWITZ**
*The Manuscript* — 27

**RICHARD SCHIFFMAN**
*Slow River* — 29
*Pointers from Scheharezade* — 30
*Rio Grande Gorge* — 32

**WENDY BROWN-BÁEZ**
*Lifelines* — 33

**LEONORE HILDEBRANDT**
*Absences* — 38
*After Crossing "Time" Off My List* — 39
*On Further Inspection* — 40

**RANDY MINNICH**
*I Think That I Shall Never See* — 42
*T'ai Chi Time* — 43

## II. ILLNESS

**PATRICIA CANNON**
*Between the Silences* — 46

**LAURIE KLEIN**
*Bridge* — 47

MARK BARKAWITZ
   *Ten Years, Huh?*     51
STEPHANIE HART
   *Only Now*     52
ANNA STEEGMANN
   *In a Silent Way*     56
ARLENE GAY LEVINE
   *The Waiting Room*     58
   *The Art of Fire Making*     60
PATTY SOMLO
   *Raisins*     61
PAUL HOSTOVSKY
   *The Air Between*     65
   *Quits*     66
   *Malingering*     67
   *The Hurt Itself*     68

## III. TRAUMA

BETH CHRISTENSEN
   *Twenty-Five Years*     72
EDWARD A. DOUGHERTY
   *Fit for Heaven*     80
KEVIN BROWN
   *Saving the Music*     83
TONY HOZENY
   *Safe for Now*     90
CHRIS ELLERY
   *Silent*     93
   *A Small Blue Flame*     94
MARY JUMBELIC
   *That Kid*     96

## IV. QUOTIDIAN

### *WONDER AT THE SMALL CONNECTIONS*

RICHARD LEBLOND
   *The Natural Moment*     106

**BONNI CHALKIN**
   *A Breath in Time* — 109

**LENORE BALLIRO**
   *Pausing* — 110

**RUSS ALLISON LOAR**
   *Zero* — 112
   *A Purple Shoelace* — 113
   *All I Know About Love I Leave* — 114
   *Quiet Moments* — 115

**MARY KAY RUMMEL**
   *Winter Solstice in Big Sur* — 116

**TERRY DALRYMPLE**
   *Our Vast and Present Moment* — 118

## IDENTITY

**JAMES SILAS ROGERS**
   *Listening at the Ragged Edge of Spring* — 124

**MOLLY RIVKIN**
   *The Girl with Upside Down Eyes* — 128

**ROBERT SPIEGEL**
   *Layered in Shadow* — 133

**SIDNEY STEVENS**
   *Two-Minute Warning* — 140

**SHERRY SHAHAN**
   *Loitering* — 149

**MURALI KAMMA**
   *Learning the Game* — 152

**LAURA REDFORD**
   *Retired* — 160

## V. PANDEMIC

### THE WAY WE LIVE NOW

**CLAUDE CLAYTON SMITH**
   *A Fresher Clime* — 166

**LAURA APOL**
   *Ode to the Heron* — 170
   *Six Suites for Unaccompanied Cello* — 172

**KRISTY SNEDDEN**
    *Babble*      *173*
    *Raven Cliffs*      *174*

**LAURA SHOVAN**
    *Pandemic Morning*      *175*
    *Walking Back from the Mailbox*      *176*
    *Waiting Room*      *177*

**ZOE SINGER**
    *Intermission*      *178*
    *And We*      *179*

**LOIS BAER BARR**
    *Thursday Morning Reflection*      *180*

**SHARON D. SHELTZER**
    *Life in a Dumpster*      *184*

**GAYLORD BREWER**
    *In Time of Crisis and Quarantine*      *190*
    *Manoir Sur-le-Cap*      *191*
    *Darkness*      *192*
    *Tomorrow Would Be a Long Day*      *193*

**LOU STOREY**
    *Inviting Sanctuary*      *194*

**MICHAEL HETTICH**
    *A Sharper Shadow*      *198*
    *Certain Harmonies*      *199*
    *Palimpsest*      *200*
    *The River*      *201*

## *A MOMENT IN HISTORY*

**MK PUNKY**
    *Pandemic (Trust)*      *204*
    *Pandemic (How Long)*      *205*
    *Pandemic (Connections)*      *206*
    *Pandemic (Possibilities)*      *207*

**DEBORAH SCHMEDEMANN**
    *Puzzling*      *208*

ALISON STONE
    *What If I Admit I Like It*      *211*
    *Herd*      *212*
    *Shelter in Place*      *213*

MARY E. KENDIG
    *How I Spent My Pandemic Vacation*      *214*

KRISTY SNEDDEN
    *Dancing with Virginia*      *220*
    *Kudzu*      *221*

NICHOLAS SAMARAS
    *Journal in the Plague Year*      *223*

ACKNOWLEDGMENTS      *238*

CONTRIBUTORS      *240*

EDITORS/PUBLISHERS      *250*

# HEATHER TOSTESON

## *THE POWER OF THE PAUSE:*
### *THE WONDER OF OUR HERE & NOW*

> *Human freedom involves our capacity to pause between the stimulus and response and, in that pause, to choose the one response toward which we wish to throw our weight. The capacity to create ourselves, based upon this freedom, is inseparable from consciousness or self-awareness.*
> —Rollo May, *The Courage to Create*

One of my favorite activities has always been to lie on the floor and watch shadows—or light—dance across a blank wall. I can do this for extended periods of time. It always feels stabilizing and replenishing. And mysterious. This moment when I am pure perception. Willing perception. The world is moving, obviously, or the shadows wouldn't be flickering. But I'm not and yet I am in full resonance with something transformed and transformative beyond me. I feel both choice and flow have been returned to me.

It is impossible to think about pause—a temporary stop—without thinking about flow, about inertia, about the arc of an action. Pause takes its meaning from what comes before and what comes after. Something that had its own incremental momentum has either exhausted itself—contradicted itself—or met something with equal or greater power, gravitas.

Pause makes us conscious of flow—the gift of flow. What it feels like to be carried along, lifted, propelled. Relieved of conscious choice. The psychologist Mihaly Csikszentmihalyi describes creative flow as a state of great joy, "a state in which people are so involved in an activity that nothing else seems to matter; the experience is so enjoyable that people will continue to do it even at great cost, for the sheer sake of doing it." Even mundane flow, the propulsion of habit, has a pleasure and an economy to it. Pause disrupts that.

Pause insists on consciousness and choice because to restart an action requires energy and awareness. This is true whether the pause is voluntary or involuntary. Pulled out of flow, we can't assume inertial, unconscious continuity. In that way restarting after pause is implicating. We're responsible now in a way we weren't before. A writer who chooses to take up a story she has put aside after an initial rush of inspiration is doing so with a different understanding of it, a different quality of engagement and commitment than she had when she first started it. The writing may well be richer, the structure clearer, for the pause. It may also feel like much harder work until something mysterious comes to meet and lift her again.

But the voluntariness or involuntariness of the pause is key to how we respond to it. A voluntary pause can result in replenishment, appreciation, deeper commitment or constructive re-evaluation, redirection—all of which provide a sense of affirmation, of truing ourselves. An involuntary pause, one we had no conscious hand in, can feel like a block—a complete, unanticipated, and unpleasant full stop—and, indeed, it is until we are in flow again. The involuntariness can make us feel helpless, vulnerable, betrayed. Even when we are in flow again, we have a different understanding of that flow. It is both more precious and more fragile. The effort required to create that new momentum can feel necessary but not necessarily affirming of our deepest needs or essential goals. It doesn't always build confidence or trust—in ourselves or in others.

The pandemic created an involuntary pause for most of us. For many it felt like, or was, a full stop. A terrifying and unanticipated one. We got sick, or the people we loved most did. We lost jobs, offices, fixed work hours, child care. We lived with increased demands and increased uncertainty, mortal threat.

Personally, the seclusion the pandemic required fitted us as introverts, made us aware of the spaciousness of our home, the gift of intimacy, the pleasure of work that we could continue without disruption, work that involves return, thoughtfulness, and communications with others based on those qualities. This, of course, was not true for our adult children who were essential workers or who constantly juggled complex careers and childcare, who found themselves questioning their current job commitments or long-term career goals.

However, this involuntary pause in all our personal lives was not accompanied by a social or cultural one. In a world that is moving faster and faster, where we can tweet and retweet in seconds, the pandemic made us hyper-communal in the abstract, electronically twitchy, intellectually overloaded and emotionally flooded, volatile and reactive. We began to re-evaluate our communal arc—and our roles in it. A shared existential threat, Covid, pushed us farther apart, not closer together. Demonstrations, protests, contested elections, endless vitriol and denunciations right and left. Often social outrage overcame health concerns. We wanted to share our visceral outrage with other bodies.

The meaning of a pause is determined by what comes after. We don't even know if it is one—and not a full stop—until life begins to flow again. And when we rejoin that flow, we rejoin it differently—consciously, implicated. Sometimes feeling more empowered. Sometimes less. In general, this societal pause appears to have had an exponentially polarizing effect. We focused most, sometimes exclusively, on what divided us as a country—and many have reentered the flow with, and through, those more hostile assumptions. We have come out of the pandemic feeling highly vulnerable to, and enraged by, forces beyond our control and also acutely aware of the preciousness and precariousness of life, our life.

So there we have it. Appreciation, vulnerability, grievance, vengeance. It is enough to give one pause.

Luckily, this collection is highly weighted toward the appreciative, the empowering. Writers in general are an introverted group. Many expanded into the gift of the pause—the time it takes to smell a rose, outwait a heron, cherish our families, understand our life choices, embrace the great good gift of existence. Implicit in many of these writings is the question of how we might make these brief, redeeming insights into a way of life. That question, of course, is at the heart of the anthology itself.

In our first section, *Meditation*, many writers failing to quiet their minds learned how to celebrate the irrepressibility of mental flow. Others assured us it was really possible to tamp the flood or just quietly attune to it. Many of the stories in the second section, *Illness*, explore what it means to live fully and gracefully in the pause that is remission. In the third section, *Trauma*, writers explore the pause that allows for grace, ways consciousness stops, or repeats, until we can faithfully integrate the intolerable—whether it is sexual abuse, the loss of a child, a tragic mistake. The fourth section, *Quotidian*, looks at how pause increases the wonder and replenishment of our small connections with nature and daily life, also at how, as individuals, we weave all the disparate moments of our lives into a sense of sustained identity. In the fifth and final section, *Pandemic*, writers explore their new normal during the pandemic, learning to play a violin, solving puzzles, changing jobs, emptying houses, while others explore the pandemic as a unique moment in history.

We found creating this anthology deeply encouraging at a time of increasing polarization. We hope you do as well. We all have the freedom, in involuntary and voluntary pauses, to choose the response toward which we throw our weight. This choice does define us. We throw it again, as a press and as individuals, towards what unites us, actively encouraging that communal flow that finds the *we* in *them*, the *us* in *you*. We all need to *imagine* better. Social media is not working for us as a redemptive imaginal space. Far from it. We need to imagine people are more like us than not, imagine that we are all vulnerable to involuntary pause and human awkwardness and need and disease and death and loss, all buffeted by circumstances beyond our control, and all committed to discovering, and rediscovering, our true north. This imagining isn't a solution, but it is a start, and is in itself a valuable and gracious practice. It is one you see repeated again and again in all the work collected here. Please join us . . .

# I
# MEDITATION

# KATHIE GIORGIO

## *SITTING*

Abigail was tired of being called a hamster. She'd been thrown onto those squeaky metal wheels ever since she was a child and in the gifted and talented program. The school specialists told her parents that while it took most people at least thirty-three repetitions to learn something new, it took Abigail only twice, and so she needed greater volume and pace to her education. Her mind was thrown into the habitrail then and onto the wheel and she'd been rolling ever since.

"I can see the gears turning," people at work said.

"Turn that brain off, turn it off!" friends said when they landed on opposing teams in Trivial Pursuit or Risk or sat opposite her in chess.

"When do you even sleep?" everyone said when she spoke of happily attending seminars, workshops, taking classes in the arts, going to lectures and readings. Recently, she went to one of those new paint-while-you-drink-wine places, because then she could learn something new and be a social drinker at the same time. Learning never went down on the value curve for Abigail. She, and her hamster, were always on the hunt. Always on the wheel.

But everyone was right, too; she and the hamster didn't sleep. Now, at fifty-two years old, it was beginning to bother Abigail. A part of her was starting to circle, looking for rest. Permanent? She didn't think so. Just some quiet time. She looked at blank walls and felt envious.

"Maybe you should try meditation," her best friend Sarah said. Sarah, whose mind was active too, but more in a bloodhound sort of way, followed at a slower pace in Abigail's wake since they were both twenty-four years old. On vacations, Abigail and her hamster went on tours and lecture series; Sarah parked the bloodhound in a kennel and took herself to resorts and spas. Abigail envied her too, though not so much her bloodhound, and so she truly considered her friend's suggestion. Meditation, she thought. The act of not thinking.

Quiet time.

And so she tried. When she sat cross-legged in front of the French doors to her deck and closed her eyes, to take advantage of the spring sun warming her skin, her eyes cracked right back open and she noticed the windows were dirty and so she stood and washed them. When she moved out in the yard and sat in the garden, her eyes betrayed her again and she noticed an anomaly in the pattern of colors in the flowers and so she got up, went to the garden store, and bought purples and blues to balance everything out. The next day, she upped her meditation strategy and tried thwarting her eyes by sitting in a dark room, shades drawn, lights out, and a sleep mask tugged over her face. But then her other senses revolted on the side of vision. She felt the grime of the carpet beneath her and she smelled that the garbage can needed emptying and so she vacuumed and emptied and then rearranged the room in a more aesthetically pleasing and balanced way.

There seemed to be no shutting down. When Abigail tried to shut down, she opened up, along with her eyes, and this brought in more tasks and problems that would itch until she overcame them.

In hamster-style, in Abigail-style, and in frustration, Abigail decided to take a class. Meditation 101. It seemed ridiculous to her, really, that anyone would have to take a class in how to sit quietly and let her mind hold still. Why would that be so difficult? But for Abigail, and for her hamster, it was.

The class was held in a "mindfulness studio" that felt a bit intimidating. It was set back from a main highway outside of town. While it was surrounded by trees and there was a large green field out back, the sound of traffic and urban life was still right there in the parking lot. Abigail hesitated beside her car, her back to the road, her face toward the building, and she debated going in. If she went inside, she thought, she would sit in silence with others, the reverberation of a starting gong telling them to sink into a void of thought, and if anything entered her mind, it should be about the homework she assumed she'd have to do. As a result, in a roundabout way, she would meditate.

If she went home, if she gave in to the intimidation, it would be just another meditation failure. Before she even sat. Before she even closed her eyes.

Abigail went inside.

She was impressed with the room. It was long, narrow and well-balanced with one full wall of windows facing the green field. The other walls were painted a restful sky blue. There were chairs for those who weren't comfortable sitting on the floor, and cushions for those who were. Abigail was going to choose a cushion until she saw a man in yoga pants sit down and tuck his legs easily into the lotus position. He began rolling his shoulders in such a loose sway that Abigail just knew he could tilt himself forward and press his nose to the floor between those two lotused knees. Quickly, Abigail chose a chair in the back corner where her middle-aged comfortable body could do whatever it was capable of without being noticed. And without being compared, she hoped.

There was tea, she saw, being served in cups without handles. Everyone spoke softly and wore soft clothes and Abigail intuited that they were speaking about deep things, slow things, contemplative things that her hamster mind, in its rush to know it all, would vault over and leave behind. When the class started, it was led by a man who lowered himself easily onto the cushions. He wore a mic so his soft voice reached every corner without coming across as loud at all. He elongated and concaved his Os in such a way that reminded Abigail of poets in coffee shops, reciting from heart while gazing earnestly at the rafters.

Those Os always made Abigail want to laugh. She wondered if the teacher wrote poetry. She bet he did, and that it had rainbows with concave Os. Butterflies too. Then she quickly shoved that thought out of her head with the teacher's admonition that it was time to close their eyes. They were going to experiment, he said. First try without any instruction at all.

"If a thought bubbles up," he said, "just notice it. Then let it float away." Then he hit the glass bowl in front of him with a little glass hammer. The chime resonated in the room, just the way Abigail imagined it would.

Okay, Abigail thought. Bubbles. Float.

Which made her think of the Os again which made her smile and snort a little. Quickly, she covered it with a throat-clearing as if she was trying to get comfortable. Which she was.

Mr. Lotus, she noticed, already had a straight spine. His eyes were closed. His palms were open on his knees. She wondered why anyone who could so easily take to the lotus position would be in a beginning class. He clearly wasn't a beginner.

Show-off, Abigail thought, then realized the class was silent and still. Everyone had their eyes closed, including the instructor. So Abigail closed hers too and tried not to move, to shift, to sway, to scratch, tried not to think, but if she did think, she thought of her thought as a bubble and tried to make it float away.

*Sitting*, she thought. Bubble.

*Sitting . . . shiva.*

What? Abigail noticed that bubble and wondered why it was there. She wasn't Jewish. Yes, she was sitting, but why would she think of sitting shiva?

And then the bubbles spewed out behind the hamster in the wheel like flatulence gone rogue rodent. Soapsuds everywhere, nearly tripping the little hamster feet that turned the metal wheel into a fan. *Sitting shiva. Jewish people sitting shiva in the lotus position. Jewish people sitting shiva in the lotus position in a room where the mirrors were covered and they couldn't see themselves sitting shiva.* Then, in her head, Abigail heard, "Shalom," with that elongated concave O and she lost it. Her laughter insulted into the room like the farts of bubbles going on in her head. Eyes opened and Abigail slapped her hand over her mouth, even though she wasn't supposed to move. But the laughter forced itself around her fingers and she wasn't supposed to laugh either. It was nervous laughter, she knew that, but it was clear it wasn't going to stop. So she kept her eyes open, put both hands over her mouth, and quickly fled the room.

She howled in the hallway and all the way down the steps. Then she promptly felt bad and went home. Another meditation failure. The hamster, trotting steadily in his wheel, hung his head.

෴ ෴ ෴

But the meditation bug just wouldn't let her go. Intellectually, meditation made sense. Abigail wanted her hamster mind to have quiet time and meditation provided that quiet. She just had to learn how. She began to approach meditation with an athlete's focus and obsession. She read books on it. She watched videos. She listened to Oprah and Deepak wield deep thoughts and stock phrases. Her mantra as she sat on the floor, or her recliner, reclined, or her recliner, straight up, or her deck, her bed, her favorite spot on the bank of the Fox River, became, "Meditate, gosh darn it! Meditate, gosh darn it!"

At lunch, her best friend Sarah said, after hearing all of these paroxysms, "What are you doing?"

Abigail took a sip of her coffee and wondered if she should switch to tea. If she should find out what they were all drinking at Meditation 101 in those little handleless cups. "Trying to learn how to meditate."

"Okay." Sarah was having a triple shot extra hot latte. Her bloodhound was tired that day. "Why?"

"Well." Abigail looked at her fingers, twisted and twined around her coffee cup. "To relax. To find inner peace?" She thought of Deepak and Oprah. "To slow down," she said honestly. "My head's too full. You know. Hamster wheel. To just—" she shrugged, "feel better."

"And are you?"

"No," Abigail said. Then she put on a concave O and repeated, "No," which made her smile and her friend laugh. But Abigail's fingers tightened. "I haven't figured out how to yet. It's harder than it looks."

Sarah hefted her latte. "It almost seems like you're either trying to earn a PhD in meditation, without practicing anything that you're learning about, or like you're in training for an Olympic competition. Like you want to be the best damn meditator there is and has been ever."

Meditate, gosh darn it. "I just want to know *how*."

"Abigail." Sarah leaned forward. "Sit. Close your eyes. Don't think."

Abigail nodded. But how to do that when the hamster in her mind had a mind of his own?

෴ ෴ ෴

So Abigail continued her quest. She listened to guided meditations. But the voices were often laconic and rolling and Abigail found herself falling asleep. Meditation was supposed to be relaxing, but was she supposed to sleep? Was there enlightenment in an afternoon nap? She didn't think so.

She read about moving meditation and so she google-searched out a labyrinth, located in one of the state parks in a town a few miles away. Set under trees and next to a different leg of her favorite river, it was a beautiful place. Abigail removed her shoes and walked barefoot on the nicely trimmed grass between the rocks lining the labyrinth path. But the hamster didn't stop, didn't even slow his pace on the wheel. Instead, the sound of the river poured in and the wildflowers captured every rapturous glance. Abigail kept stopping to admire the colors around her, to compare and contrast their frequency and intensity, to listen and revel and decipher the sounds and scents. As she sat on the meditation bench, which Abigail determined was in the exact center of the labyrinth, her mind filled with lightplay and color, percentages and intensity ranges, patterns and skips. She and her hamster went home feeling full, but also a failure again. This wasn't what meditation was supposed to be about.

Abigail called the mindfulness studio again and arranged for a one on one session with a different instructor. She sat in front of him, face to face, in the room with the wide windows and skyblue wall. He faced the windows, she faced the wall. He instructed her to close her eyes. She did. Then he led her through six deep breaths, in through her nose, out through her mouth, and she did. Then he said they were going to sit in silence for ten minutes and she was to try to hold still the entire time. Hold still and not think.

"If you feel a muscle wanting to move, just notice it, then let it go," he said. He told her the bubble story too, with a variation. "If a thought comes up, look at it for a moment, and then picture a balloon. Tie your thought on the string of that balloon and then watch them both float away."

To her relief, the instructor didn't use the concave Os. And Abigail liked balloons, especially red ones. So she felt hopeful as she closed her eyes. The instructor hit the glass bowl with the little glass hammer and the sound that rang out was clear and shivered and made Abigail have a thought—that chime was what her hope would sound like. But she wasn't supposed to be thinking. So she put her hope and the sound on the string of a red balloon and pictured them floating away.

Within a few moments, one eye opened, then the other. She looked at the face of her instructor. He sat serene, his face smooth, his breathing even. She wondered if he used any anti-wrinkle cream or if his youthful face was the result of years of meditation. Of thoughts floating away in balloons. Maybe as the mind emptied of thoughts, the skin emptied of the capacity to wrinkle. She wondered how he would know when the ten minutes were up. She looked down at the glass bowl and couldn't discern any timer attached to it. She couldn't find a clock anywhere in the room.

She began to study the way the sunlight played on the blue of the walls. Abigail wondered and predicted how the color would change as the shadow of sunset fell in, followed by the dark of the night sky. Would the moonlight affect it? Where would the moon be? In what phase and how would the phase affect the light? What about clouds? But then she noticed the light on the wall was like ripples on a stream. Like the river at the labyrinth. Like the river near her home where she liked to walk. Like blue. Just blue. Blue and blank. Blue and blue and more blue . . .

When the time, apparently ten minutes, passed and the instructor opened his eyes to hit the closing gong on the bowl, he found Abigail, her eyes wide open. "Abigail," he said, his voice soft, but she swore she heard the slightest exasperation, "your eyes are supposed to be closed. Did you have them open the whole time?"

"Almost. I suppose I did," she admitted.

"You suppose?"

"I don't really remember. I got sort of lost in the blue. I'm sorry. I just wasn't thinking."

As Abigail left that afternoon, she felt like a failure all over again. She'd flunked at the most basic thing—keeping her eyes closed for ten minutes. She'd also gone well past her usual repetition of two times before learning. She wasn't learning. She wondered if her brain was broken. If she was missing the meditation gene in her DNA. She wondered if in this case, her hamster was running with a limp.

※ ※ ※

After parking her car, Abigail just didn't feel like going into her home. It seemed like everywhere she looked now, there was a reminder of her failure. Her windows. Her garden. Her deck, her bedroom, her living room, all of it. Who knew that not thinking could be so difficult? Who knew that not thinking could be an accomplishment?

*Abigail's mind learns quickly,* her teachers said. *Abigail needs greater volume and pace to her education.*

She thought of a blank wall and sighed.

Tucking her hands in her pockets, Abigail walked down the street and took the turns she knew by heart to her favorite spot. Her city had a Riverwalk, a lovely stroll next to the Fox River. Mostly urban, the Riverwalk had a point where it trailed away from the downtown and into the woods, dousing the walker with the rural in a few short steps.

Before moving into the woods, Abigail glanced at times over the cobblestones and down the bank and into the sunsparkled river. But mostly, she watched her feet. She thought how it really wasn't a bad thing to think. Thinking was good. It brought ideas and theories and plans and inventions. She remembered when she was praised for the hamster in her head, when empty-headed was a bad thing to be. But somehow, as she grew older, hamsters and wheels became negative. You were supposed to relax, to not think, to connect with the great mystery of the universe by simply becoming a part of it.

There was nothing simple about it.

Abigail liked to think. She didn't like being compared to a hamster, but the hamster had been with her for her entire life. He got her where she was. He got her where she was going. He was a pet that ran through the labyrinth of her habitrail brain.

So who cared if she couldn't meditate? The hamster didn't.

But Abigail did. She wanted to circle. She wanted to rest.

Abigail walked and looked at her feet. The cobblestones gave over to gravel and the sounds of the city to softness. The light became diffused and dappled, flitting over the gravel and sending sparks of warmth onto Abigail's cheeks and scalp.

And then it brightened when Abigail stepped into the spot where the river widened, demanding more space, and where the trees obediently fell back, allowing grass to grow and the full strength of the sun to encompass. Abigail shuddered from pure pleasure at the heat. She stepped toward the river, watched the waltz of sun and current, and then she looked up.

Oh, the blue. The vibrant and cascading soft blues of the sky. Wide. Flat. Lit somehow from within. Abigail opened her eyes wide into the blue and the blank and the entire world fell into her gaze. She leaned into the sky, slack-jawed, open-eyed, and fell thoughtless into the blue and the blue and the blue.

For untold minutes. Without a gong to start. Without a gong to stop.

Though when she got a crick in her neck, Abigail blinked. She also found that she'd sunk to a sit on the banks of the river and her comfortable body had its legs comfortably crossed. As she looked out over the water, her hand massaging the back of her neck, she didn't have a thought in her head.

Not a one.

Gradually, birdsong began to register and she heard the whisper and occasional declarative of the river. The sun warmed her shoulders and dazzled her view. And she relaxed into a smile. Her hamster yawned and stretched.

I did it, she thought. Bubble. Balloon.

She watched that thought float in a triumph of red over the river.

Then Abigail stood, did her own full body stretch, and walked home. She wondered how many gallons of water were rushing by her, how many fish were there, was there a ratio, did they come out more when there was sun, did fish who swam in the sun taste better than fish who swam in the shade. The hamster trotted beside her inside her. And she kept her eyes open wide, looking for the next blank, the next blue, the whole way.

## DIANE ELAYNE DEES

### *THE SPACE WITHIN*

*a sonnet for Patricia*

The space within each breath, we seldom notice,
like the moment that the dusk turns into night,
or the creeping cloud that softly dims the light.
We step around the mud that births the lotus,
afraid to get our feet wet. We are stranded
on an island we created from our fear,
surrounded by an ocean of despair.
And so, we tell ourselves that we're abandoned;
we forget to note the space within each breath.
With one foot in the future and the other
in the past, we tell ourselves that we would rather
deny our birth, bring on our spirit's death.
The space within each breath is always there,
inviting us to pause, become aware.

## SACRED CIRCLE

When the student is ready,
the teacher will appear—
when the teacher is ready,
the lesson will appear—
when the lesson is ready,
the circumstance will appear—
when the circumstance is ready,
the student will appear.

## *TASTE*

A yogi told me
that, before I speak,
I should focus
on the tip of my tongue.
All these sweet taste buds
await my attention,
ready to deliver satisfying
answers, delicate questions,
mere confections of opinion.

## NADEL HENVILLE

### *CATHOLICISM + ADHD*

As soon as I learned how to talk, I had to learn how to pray. It was a requirement of Catholicism, it's in the Ten Commandments, and Jesus probably mentions it a few times in the New Testament.

Or at least that's what I'm told.

Just learn the *Our Father,* the *Hail Mary,* and you'll be fine. Maybe even try to throw in a prayer to your future husband St. Michael, so you don't disappoint eleven-year-old you. Repeat them every single day, without reprieve, and maybe, just *maybe,* you'll feel what it was like to have God watching over you every day.

Oh, and bonus! You probably won't burn in eternal fire and brimstone. Keep praying, don't stop. If you stop, you'll sin. If you pause, you're a sinner. Don't pause to understand the words you're saying, don't stop to think about what your faith will actually mean. Don't stop.

※ ※ ※

"Our Father, who art in heaven, hallowed be thy name—"

*The floor is way too cold beneath my knees, I should sit on my bed for this . . . But if I sit on my bed because I didn't want cold knees, what does that say that Jesus could have literal nails shoved into his tendons for me and I sat while I asked him for . . . what is it, "help"?*

*Wait, what did I say?*

"Hallowed be thy name—"

*Hallowed. Ha-llowed. Is that another word for holy? "Oh, how holy is thy name." That makes more sense than hallow, lowkey it sounds like Halliwell from* Charmed, *which was a good show—*

"Thy will be done, on earth—"

*They talk a lot about "All Hallows Eve."*

. . .

*Should I have been watching a show about witches and demons? That sounds like the opposite of what a Christian would do.*

*I mean, to be fair, I didn't know, and I really liked the way Chris Halliwell looked—and his brother Wyatt. But really, only when he has long hair, which technically was when Wyatt was evil—*

*Oh my God is that where my "I can fix him" complex comes from?*

*Oof, I shouldn't be saying God like that!*

I don't stop. I can't stop. Fire and brimstone are seconds away from the back of my neck, and if I stop then I'm done for. If I stop praying, stop talking, stop *saying something* then I'm more lost than I thought I was in the first place, and then I have to focus on what chemotherapy means for my mother, and what morphine does, and why she looks smaller than she did before. If I stop praying, then I'm messing up my last chance to know her in another life—to know her again, to love her again and to feel her again.

I should be praying.

"Sorry Jesus. My bad. I'll just—I'll start over. Hail Mary, full of grace, the Lord is with thee—"

*Haha, that sounds like a prophecy. "The Lord is with thee Mary."*

*I know Mary is visiting her sister . . . or cousin? . . . Elizabeth, who's pregnant with John the Baptist, and when they see Mary, they're like "Woo! The Savior's here!" And—did Jesus talk to John telepathically? Were they best friends in heaven? And did Mary have a perfect pregnancy? Like did she still have morning sickness and cravings and sore feet and did her hormones change a lot, was she ever really hungry and not get her cravings or did God always provide? Did the birth hurt?? I wish I asked Mummy.*

"Holy Mary, mother of God, pray for us sinners, now and at the hour of our death. Amen."

*So glad this asks her to pray for us because I think I'm royally fucking this up.*

SHIT I'M SORRY JESUS SORRY MY BAD FORGIVE ME FOR MY SINS.

Walking away is easier than it should be when she's no longer here. Though my mother's passed on everything she knew about Christianity, and I hold on tight enough to remember there's a place we'll meet again, the *Our Father* becomes a chore, the *Hail Mary* becomes automatic, and St. Michael breaks up with me because I stood him up on every date we had.

The fire I'm supposed to have leaves. And though there's a little bit of *something* there, I don't notice it's gone until I pretend I'm conveniently sick every time Sunday at 8 a.m. rolls around. King James' version of the Bible makes absolutely *no sense* anymore (not that it ever did), and the weird side looks from the priest makes me more uncomfortable than it did when I was a preteen.

Catholicism gets sketchier, and so Catholic College feels like the next natural step.

Passing by the chapel feels like I'm passing by Jesus in a hallway, and we both side eye each other because we know we saw the other, but we don't know if we're good enough acquaintances to warrant a random wave, and so we either give that weird tight-lipped-dad-smile and never look at each other again, or I pretend my phone got *really* interesting and I just didn't see a dude in B.C. Middle-Eastern robes standing in front of me.

It takes the constant itching of *something* that never went away for me to understand what it might mean. An English Standard Version of the Bible coincidentally ends up in my room, and the campus priest looks at me like a person.

I start saying hi to the out-of-time Son of God in front of the chapel, because it seems we're friends again. And he smiles at me like we always were—and that he's been waiting.

When it's time to *pray*, I think I know how. It's only a bonus that St. Michael seems to have never gotten over me, so each night the Holy words I learned as a child pour out of my mouth like I never stopped.

But . . . the more I pray the farther I feel.

"St. Michael the archangel, defend us in battle. Be our safeguard against the wickedness and snares of the devil. May God rebuke him, we humbly pray. And do thou oh prince of the heavenly host—"

*Heyyy look at me focusing. I finally almost got through a prayer, I just gotta get through the rest of it. But I'm focusing!! I'm focusing real good.*

... Is it because it's a prayer to St. Michael? Am I focusing this hard because of our eventual marriage?? Is that idolatry? I should literally be paying attention to Jesus, not an Angel who doesn't call me back.

*I wonder if St. Michael is as terrifying as the Bible makes the other Angels out to be.*

"Be not afraid." Haha.
*Be afraid. Be very afraid.*
"Amen."
*Amen?*
*Amen.*
*What did I miss?*
*What did I miss?*
*What am I doing wrong?*
"Jesus, forgive me—"
*Faith shouldn't be this hard—it was never this hard before, why can't I focus and get through this and actually get to a place I want to be why can't I focus why can't I focus why can't I focus—*
"Jesus, *help me.*"
**That's all you needed to ask.**
Shoving my face into my bed is what allows me to actually breathe.
And I stop.
And wait.
And breathe.
And *breathe.*
And settle.
And *laugh.*
*God gave me ADHD for a reason—and since I gotta live my life with him, it's gonna be* both *of our problems.*
**As it should be.**
"Here's the thing—I know right from wrong when I'm here at the end of the day after prancing around and being a menace, but why can't I fix the things I need to in the moment so I don't hurt anyone or hurt *you?* And **yes, I know that I just need to pause** but it's almost impossible, my mind goes a mile a minute and I have at least sixty songs on loop in my head all at once, **and I try to have them be gospel songs all the time,** but how do I know what I'm doing will get me closer to you when I take a step forward and like twelve steps back? It was never this hard in the beginning, and though I did annoy

Mummy ninety percent of the time while we were at church, why can't I have her determination? Her faith? Why isn't this easy? Half of me talking to you is ranting **and I know I shouldn't compare my faith to others, because that'll drive me away again,** but how am I supposed to get better when all I do is focus on other things?"

. . .

. . .

**One day at a time.**
*Okay.*

"And another thing, I got some questions to ask you—well Mary really and Elizabeth if she can come to the phone right now, and if she's not busy, how about St. Michael—"

# JAMES WYSHYNSKI

## *MEDITATION WITH TWO VOICES*

*Come back to breath.*
        *Be a screen door. What's left*
                *after all passes through?*

The screen, the holes in it made by wasps,
        paint flaking, a hinge
                with a loose screw.

*A loose screw, my friend.*
        *Be a square of space*
                *in the screen.*

Deep between my shoulders,
        in vertebrae,
                in marrow—

bills, dishes, oil changes.
        A wound, opens and closes
                like a jellyfish.

Deep into my breath, it's always the same:
        Night, beach, tide pool. A small shark
                circles in its cell. Its fin

tip breaks the surface,
        wet and slick. A boy with a stick
                prods.

Then the blind man
> with a metal detector:
>> both cane and divining rod,

the metal scope that hangs
> from his waist
>> overflowing with moonlight.

## *MORNING COMMUTE, 9:17 A.M.*

As I wait out the light,
before I turn into
my office complex,
I glance down
at the concrete
island that divides
the lanes and see
a raccoon turning
unsteady circles
in a patch of burnt
grass—sick, I think,
dying, and I want
the impossible:
not turn him
into a stand-in
for me or my life,
but to see him
and his pain,
one mammal
to another, stuck
on a median
of broad leafed
weeds and sun-
scorched earth.

## LARRY LEFKOWITZ

### *THE MANUSCRIPT*

The finished manuscript lay on the desk, quiescent in the light from the full moon. It seemed to hint at some mystery beyond Kunzman's grasp. He thought of the opening paragraph of Bruno Schulz's short story, 'The Book,' in which Schulz searches for The Book that contains the answers to everything, to the meaning of life, that he remembers from his childhood. He discovers the Polish maid tearing out its pages in order to wrap meat, and when he finally rescues it from her, all that remains are the advertisements at the back.

A feeling of panic seized Kunzman—that something similar might happen to *his* book. He had the sudden urge to get the book to the publisher before some disaster befell it. Being evening, the publisher was closed.

In bed that night, he began to worry himself with tales of lost manuscripts, some of them true. I. B. Singer had brought a story to the newspaper offices of *The Forward*, but when he opened the envelope, he discovered it contained the wrong manuscript. He called home immediately, only to learn that the cleaning woman had thrown the good manuscript into the garbage. Singer improved on his experience by writing a story "Manuscript" in which Shivta, the mistress of the writer, and he flee to Warsaw at the outbreak of war with a suitcase containing the manuscript. When the suitcase is opened, it contains the manuscript of some novice writer, and the devoted Shivta walks all the way back to Warsaw to retrieve the manuscript. She finds it and returns to Bialystok with it, reaching the city early in the morning. She finds the writer in bed with another woman. Pulling out the manuscript from under her shirt, she opens the door of the oven, and tosses it in. And had not some of Singer's stories and unfinished novels been the real-life victims of a burst pipe which flooded the room in which they were kept with water and he feared they had been lost? And Singer hadn't had to contend with more modern threats, such as missiles possibly targeting his work.

Fearing a disaster to his manuscript, Kunzman slept with it near his bed, within arm's reach, waking from his fitful sleep from time to time to check on it, the odd thought that it didn't even contain advertisements as in Schulz's story to save vexed him for some reason. At one point he awoke, beads of sweat on his forehead, after dreaming that a critic dismissed his book with the Yiddish description, "*bliyendike mistn*" (manure in full bloom). At another point he dreamt that he was Gregor Samsa who awoke one morning from uneasy dreams to find himself transformed into a gigantic insect *who began to devour his book!* Awakening in horror from this nightmare, he felt a two-fold sense of relief: that he had not been transformed into an insect and, almost as important, that he hadn't lost the book.

Then a completely irrational thought assailed him: that he might die before he could deliver his book to the publisher. Timing his setting forth to bring him to the publisher precisely at the hour of opening, Kunzman carried the manuscript, feeling as if he held in his hands a sacred bird which would fly away if he relaxed his grip, declining to emulate Shivta's keeping the manuscript under her shirt for safekeeping only because he feared he would look ridiculous.

The situs of the publisher was within walking distance. And the whole way he feared some accident would befall the manuscript. Once handed over, Kunzman felt as if he had shed a great weight. An almost epiphanic joyfulness enveloped him. Yes, a time for celebration.

That night, unable to sleep, Kunzman imagined himself the alter ego to the young Dostoevsky after the latter delivered his first book *Poor Folk* to his editor. The editor had read it all night until, unable to restrain his enthusiasm for it any longer, he went to the author's residence, despite its being four o'clock in the morning, to inform him of his greatness. The next day he delivered the manuscript to a known literary critic and announced to him "a new Gogol is born!"

## RICHARD SCHIFFMAN

*SLOW RIVER*

All day long racing around
like molasses on steroids,
all day long spinning your whorls
like a punch-drunk flower.

When the bird calls your cellphone,
it always gets a busy signal.
That tree's been rooting for you all along.
But you're the flapping cuckoo
that's got no branch to land on.

Why not be more like a slow river?
Always leaving, always arriving
exactly where you are—
now and now and now and now.
Don't call that river sluggish. You're the one
that's going nowhere / fast.

So here's what I'd suggest—
rest a spell on your metaphysical laurels.
If the world asks what you are doing,
just grin like Mona Lisa and take the Fifth.

When some crackpot cracks the whip,
leap on his lap like a newborn pup, and wither the idiot
with your gaze of fathomless peace.

## POINTERS FROM SCHEHERAZADE

We are not talking Hollywood endings.
We are talking nerve endings, live wires
spitting shards of fire—
those are the stories you'll need
to keep alive.

Spin the old boy on his toes
with your tales within tales within tales.
Dazzle him with all he cannot know.
Like geese who fly first north, then south,
change course with every season. Let your trail vanish
like deer tracks in falling snow.

Neither straighten out the kinks of plot,
nor offer any facile explanations.
The web you weave is not a highway.
The heart is not a destination.
It is a labyrinth for getting lost.

Lose yourself, therefore, in the maze
of your own telling. Lure the bat-blind Sultan
deeper. Twist him around your narrative finger.
Without a story to tell, you are dead meat.
Every cliffhanging episode will give
you something new to live for.

But take care not to get lost in your own flight.
For Houdini, the strait-jacket was not a prison,
but a vesture of escape. And the spider weaves a web,
not to catch herself, but to snag her prey.
Tread lightly, therefore, on the net you've spun.

A bridge is not a home to rest in,
but a vaulting passage to the other bank.
Sinbad sailed beyond the seven seas.
Aladdin lost the lamp, but found his soul.
Bind him who holds you hostage
in your story's dizzy twists and turns.
Then swallow him whole.

## *RIO GRANDE GORGE*

The earth puckered its lips
and the high Sierra has been pouring
its snowmelt heart there ever since.

The earth puckered its lips
and the river can't stop babbling
sea chanties to the sagebrush desert.

The earth puckered its lips
and everything tumbled in—
dragon flies, the moon, the coldly winking stars.

The earth puckered its lips
and the tourists snapped their selfies
as they teetered dizzy on that igneous brink.

The earth puckered its lips,
the hikers hiked, the rafters rafted,
the swimmers swam, the jumpers jumped.

And yes, a few just stood there gobsmacked and transfixed,
gazing at the frothing Rio, drinking in
the ceaseless, distant hiss, trying to imagine

how all that liquid bliss, had murmured on and on
six million years of summers—slicing through
the Earth's black heart of stone.

# WENDY BROWN-BÁEZ

## *LIFELINES*

Let's say that suddenly the breath is knocked out of you by shocking news. Let's say your heart is broken by loss, by unexpected change, by rejection, by remorse. Let's say you have to make a terrible decision or face your greatest fears. Or maybe to make a choice you wish you didn't have to make. Let's say you are consumed with doubt or regret, with envy or hesitation. Let's say you are trapped in a reality such as prison or a brutal marriage or in your own negative thoughts. What is the simplest way to calm the mind when it is scattered in every direction, when it is dancing a Bossa Nova of fear and dismay in your head?

Meditation.

You don't need anything but a few minutes of time. You don't need equipment, although having a meditation pillow is helpful, but a chair, a rug, or space under a tree will do. You don't need silence, although it helps to settle the mind more quickly. You don't need classes or long instructions, although they are available for strengthening your practice. And you don't need a special place, a room or building, or a group. You carry meditation with you.

My first experience of meditation was Transcendental Meditation. In 1972, when my friend enthusiastically announced that he had started to meditate, I was skeptical. After all, I was eighteen and suspicious of anything organized. "We can't stay friends if you don't learn how to meditate," he told me. He wouldn't let up until I finally gave in for the sake of our friendship. What could it hurt? Harry taught me to sit up, but I didn't need a special pose or even to sit cross-legged on the floor. (This was a huge relief to me.) I agreed to give meditation a trial run.

I had no idea that my life would change, radically and suddenly. I hadn't realized that I felt stifled by discontentment: my job after I graduated from high school bored me, my relationship with my boyfriend was unfulfilling.

Max wouldn't commit, wouldn't help with the bills yet basically lived with me. I had no idea how to be in a relationship. I wanted love but had little idea how to walk in another's shoes; I was too busy trying to stay upright in my own platforms.

I meditated dutifully for twenty minutes twice a day, during my lunch break and after dinner. At work, I sat in the storage area, drowning out the sounds in the store behind me by intoning a mantra in my head. At night, I meditated by sitting in a stuffed armchair in my tiny apartment.

Where was Max? It seems as though he came and went, sometimes staying with me for three or four days in a row, then vanishing. I had learned TM while he was at the ski resort and I continued to practice when he came back.

At first, I didn't think anything was happening. The twenty minutes made me feel energized. And clear-headed. A strange sense of discomfort grew, like wearing clothes that had grown too tight. The contrast between the inner states of peaceful awareness and the outer condition of my life pulled tauter and tauter until it snapped.

I remember dressing up to go out to a party. I remember walking the darkened streets and thinking, "I will meet someone tonight." I remember walking into the room and our eyes meeting and knowing, a tingling through my body, that here was my future.

Billy took me away from anything familiar. He had been accepted at St. John's College in Santa Fe and I demanded that he take me with him. I was ready to leave the job and the boyfriend. Meditation had shaken something awake in me. An awareness that I had to move along, take a leap of faith, try on a new life. Search for something more than what I had settled for.

Within a month we were on the road.

Before landing in Santa Fe, we stopped in San Francisco. We attended Zazen meditation practice at the Zen center, a roomful of people sitting cross-legged on snafus, the round Japanese pillows, in silence for 40 minutes. The silence was surreal, but it helped to be in a crowd or I would have given up. And yet, again, this feeling of almost about to tap into something . . . serenity, I think. In the apartment where we stayed with friends, we meditated, made love, argued, and tried to get to know each other. I was head over heels, but insecure and clingy. He was focused on his future and unsure how I fit into it.

When we reached Santa Fe, Billy broke up with me. I was completely devastated. Nothing had ever hurt so much. I sat on my cushion, twice a day.

Despite the physical discomfort of sitting (my legs bolstered with pillows), something was happening inside me. I felt centered during those moments of focused breathing, moments of freedom from emotional turmoil. I didn't have to have answers or even ask questions when I sat on the pillow and counted my breaths to ten and then to ten again.

It was the only way I could survive. My thoughts careened everywhere. Even the beauty of desert skies and mountains could not soothe the discord in my heart, a wrestling match between hope and brokenness.

When I meditated, somewhere deep within me was joy, a cascading sensation that started under my navel and went up and down to my heart. I knew it was there, even if only reachable when I sat in complete stillness and followed my breath. Even when my life was lonely and I felt insignificant and confused, those minutes were crystal clear, a bell ringing inside me that proclaimed I was spirit, I was more than unsettled desires and unpredictable feelings.

Meditation not only changed me but saved me. It was emergency medicine.

As time went by, I had relationships with lovers and friends, experimented with theater and housed and fed the homeless, and birthed sons. I traveled to the East Coast and the West Coast and to Spain and to Israel, always coming back to Santa Fe.

Meditation dropped away when the love of my life, Michael, returned to my life. He swept me off my feet with flowers, took our son under his wing. But his moods swung out of control: drinking and marijuana, risky car trips at top speed, jailed for irrational aggression when pulled over, disappearing across the border and calling me days later. Euphoria descended into depression until I felt suffocated under its heavy cloud. Where once we had been enthralled with each other, now he told me he wanted to die.

We tried everything under the sun, from acupuncture to psychodrama.

I was faced with the dilemma of the best way to cope with Michael's increasing mental instability. I thought about meditation but was afraid. I knew it would change things. I knew it would reveal my exhaustion, fear, disappointment. I knew it would force me to make decisions. It would mean a shift in perspective: from caring for his needs to taking care of mine. I teetered on the brink by praying in sweat lodges or walking medicine wheels or entering sacred ceremony but refused to go back to the daily practice.

After he died, I had to find full-time work. The position of preschool teacher made good use of my years of experience with children, although it was physically and mentally exhausting. That spring in my women's Moon Lodge I announced, "I am going to spend the entire week of spring break in meditation." The women could see how deeply tired I was. "I want to honor that," one of the women said. "I'll bring you meals so you don't even have to cook. I'll drop them at your door." I was touched by this, and humbled.

I spent time sitting and following my breath but I also chanted and danced. Alone. In tune with my inner rhythm. The state of serenity I finally entered was so delicious, I wanted it to last.

Eventually my life completely transformed, from preschool teacher to performance poet, from performing poetry to writing instructor, from Santa Fe to Minneapolis where my grandsons live. I taught in prisons, at a healing center, with teens in crisis. I know my own resiliency is bolstered from a foundation built on years of meditation practice. It enables me to leave my personality at the door for those who need my full attention. It enables me to show up with compassion. My ability to think on my feet and respond in the moment comes from meditation. It enables me to discharge the stories I hear of abuse, shame, regret, fear, and grief.

And then the great pivot when the pandemic forced us to cancel workshops, classes, readings, retreats, and events. The learning curve to use technology was steep; often I threw up my hands in frustration. I was awed by my grandson's ability to find both schoolwork and entertainment online as fast as his fingers can fly.

The pandemic gave me time for reflection. Since I was no longer taking the bus to get everywhere, hours were added to my week, not to mention less stress.

I listened to inspiring podcasts presented by spiritual teachers and writers I admire. I attended virtual readings and meetings and workshops. I was busy navigating between what was necessary for me to stay healthy and what was happening in the world. I had to consider how to cultivate moments of tranquility, to say no to unfinished projects, no matter how much they tugged on me to complete them.

But then George Floyd was killed. And the world exploded in front of my eyes.

This happened in the neighborhood where I enjoyed going out for lunch, where I attended cutting-edge theater and browsed books in a bookstore, where I took my grandsons swimming. The neighborhood, with the best tacos and the most subversive poetry reading series tucked into a tiny café, was where many of my friends lived.

Friends posted on Facebook when the protests turned into riots and they didn't feel safe in their own homes. My heart was breaking even as I was astonished at how the protests caught fire all over the world.

My leisure to think, meditate, journal, and listen to podcasts was such a gift.

What I learned during the pandemic is that we each count, we each matter. No matter what our circumstances, we can be a force for good. We needed to stop, to transform our past into hope for the future. Rather than "half full or half empty," I can see a glass that is shattered or I can see a glass that is overflowing. It depends on the angle from which I choose to look.

Through the twists and turns of a life lived on the edge, meditation is a thread that glimmers like a lifeline to sanctuary. I shut my eyes and become still; I recognize the activity of the "monkey mind" and let go. Back to the breath, over and over. Back to myself, over and over, the Self that exists no matter what else is going on. We are not our circumstances. This I remember as I breathe intentionally, settle into the vastness revealed in silence. It brings me back to knowing that I can't settle for anything less than what makes my soul sing.

# LEONORE HILDEBRANDT

## *ABSENCES*

contrary to the daily bustle
      the engagements I keep
      the lists I compile
      the setbacks
my sleepless hours are ruptures
when everything goes on
without me
      the river and its floods
      a fox skirting the field
      trains and elevators
      the notations of planets
and in the dark
I dare the briefest thought
of a life without you
      and with no house to call home
      no evening sky
      for the last time
      I have climbed the mountain
      ate my last slice of bread—
a somber exercise
this venturing into negative space
      without you
only to come back
for now
      to love's pleasure
      the good land
      my precious lungs
and I'm alive like a garden
made of wind and earth and light
      call it purity
      call it bliss

## AFTER CROSSING "TIME" OFF MY LIST

I wander around in the dark.
Rows of digital keys flicker into the night.

A woman sits on a concrete foundation.
She waves me over, whispers,
"You can have anything you want."
Her dress shimmers with conviction.

I find my pen and cross out "want."
What's next?

A street lamp casts a hooded glow.
From the gravel I pick up a stone,
then another, use spit to wake the colors—
magenta, red, orange, sienna
mined from the earth-past.

It's getting light. I start a new list.

## ON FURTHER INSPECTION

there's nothing wrong     with musing     with ruminating on the past
to witness oneself     connecting and leave-taking

I crave a more perfect union     for myself and the world
but my reflections are often cyclical     intrusive     and loud

for example     when I helped a stranger who seemed lost     I hurried
running late     I failed to give enough     (could it have been enough?)

later     stuck on thought-circles     I repeated     who said what
replaying the omissions—     without resolve     no moving on

even my dreams are loopy     a man falls     I try to call out     but no voice
I'm stalled     chewing the same cud     grazing a perpetual field of thorns

if I were president     of my affairs     I'd keep my mind-space     clear
there'd be no echoes refusing to fade     no conjuring up

more favorable outcomes     I'd be ready for the next big thing
I know it is possible     to alter settings     to get unstuck

the other day     I took a hike around two mountains     a figure eight
and the few people I met     were like friends     all of us sane     available

let's say you get up     and leave yourself     only to come back     to the same
caged animal     frenzied in circles     the same walled-in questions

until helplessness subdues motion—     there's no blueprint for escape
but for starters     ask what sets it off     a wish to be seen favorably?

on the mountain loop     I followed rocky paths     breath-happy
and getting hot     I took a game-trail to the ridge     shed layers

piled clothes on a boulder     raised my hat     turned myself
and again     to take in the valleys and hills     loosely folded around me

rumination—     when the cattle lie down     quietly
given to deep thought     toward a more perfect union

## RANDY MINNICH

### *I THINK THAT I SHALL NEVER SEE*

If trees had never grown on Earth
and photos back from Mars showed
hillsides of columnar things—
like Roman ruins with green feathers—

I might see trees—a while—astonished

that they burst right from the brick-red soil.
Maybe I'd ponder their slow determined life
from nut to gnarled crashing ruin,
their lives lived grazing on the sun.

Or maybe not. Amazement passes quickly,

for I live so swiftly down the highway
wonders such as trees tick by
like fenceposts by the roadside,
vanish in the distance, barely seen.

I should slow down.

But unlike sap, blood races on
down countless frantic inner paths
it sets itself upon and only briefly
looks beyond.

Seeing miracles takes time.

## T'AI CHI TIME

5:25—Running late.
Thirty-five minutes to drive
a journey that took forty-five.
But my teacher had said, "don't rush.
Cover the dashboard clock.
Relax your thumbs. Sink into the seat.
Breathe all the way to your fingertips."
I arrived at 5:58.

"Impossible," I muttered.
My teacher shrugged.
"That's T'ai Chi time."

The master was late in Manhattan one day.
The cabby was darting,
gap to gap,
beating the horn,
swearing through lights.
Felt a tap on his shoulder:
"I'm in a hurry.
Please slow down."

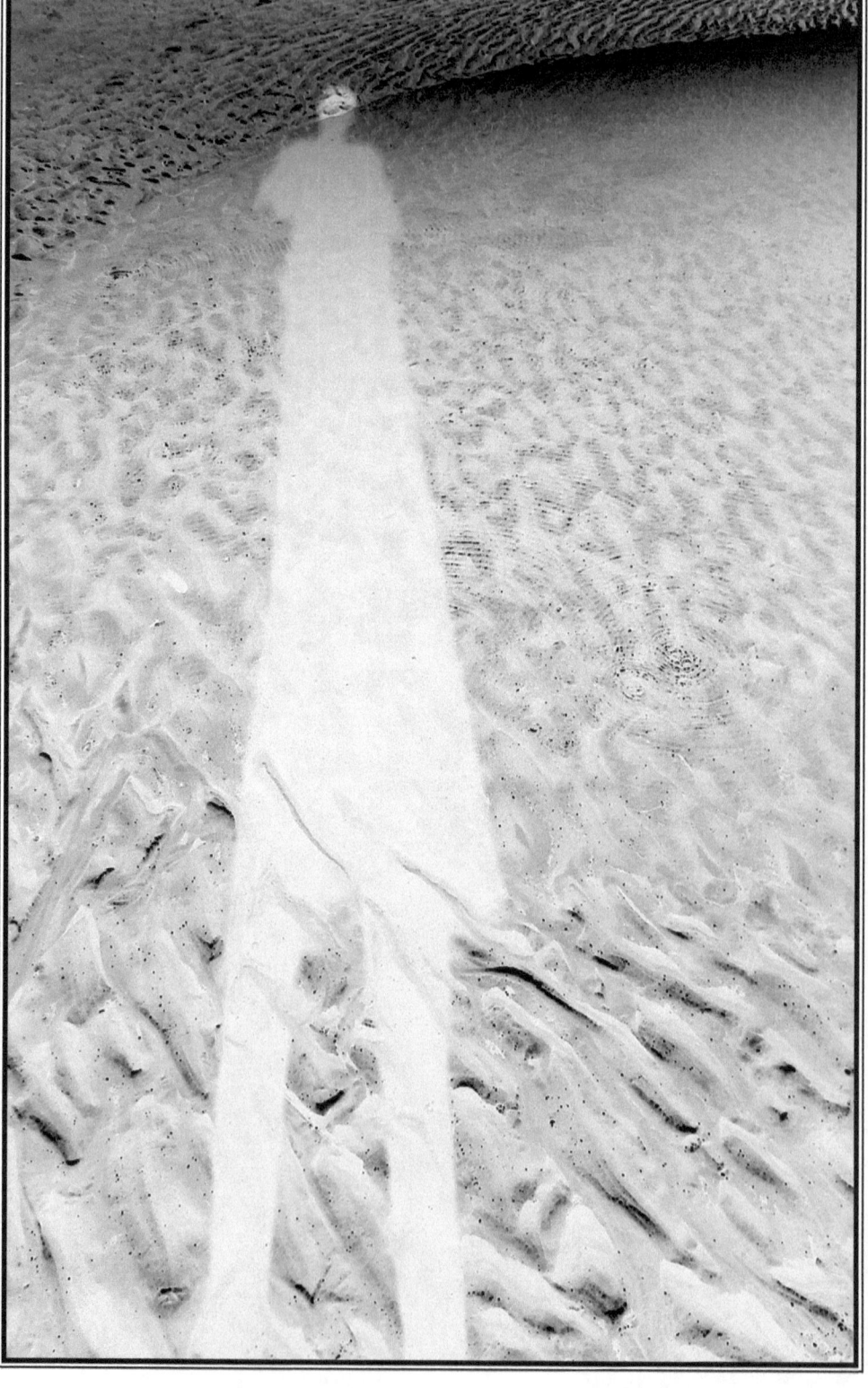

# II
# ILLNESS

# PATRICIA CANNON

## *BETWEEN THE SILENCES*

*In memory of Julie*

In December
the sky fell
white
like the sheet
that covered your face
and pressed your tired body
into the pause
   *. . . where you remain forever*
     *thirty-seven, swan-necked and*
     *swimming in sheets of music . . .*
On that day
the boxes on a calendar
collapsed and swept
its black lines
under a wave
   *. . . the sound of your fingers*
     *strumming the strings*
     *on your guitar . . .*
Mourning has long
settled and evaporated
like a gentle mist
but the memory
of your laughter persists
    *. . . like a strained note*
    *between the silences . . .*

# LAURIE KLEIN

## *BRIDGE*

> *Movement*
> *is the one reliable thing.*
> *And then it—also—moves.*
> —Jennifer Wallace

I once knew a boy with a dazzler grin: a towhead, funny and fierce as a tumbleweed.

From childhood on, Michael's fingers attracted pens, markers, brushes and paints. By day, he spun out designs: concentric, erratic, and linear. His boyish psyche seemed half-magnet, seeking patterns like iron filings.

I imagined, by night, this nephew of mine mentally swinging between high-rise towers, entrusting all to sinewy mental threads, a spiderman of his own making.

I only speculate. My role as aunt never took root. At the time, I blamed childhood ghosts.

"For every child born," an obstetrician once said, "ten thousand things have to go right."

Michael—despite those initial, vital connections—moved fitfully into adolescence. Somewhere along the line his brain jarred, as if a small, soundless explosion took out the one crucial, interior bridge. Rapids seethed below. And afterward, the sporadic collapse of reason.

I prayed for him but mostly wrote myself out of his story. His bouts with despair too closely resembled my favorite uncle's fatal path. Drugs, flashbacks, escalating distortions—the similarities unnerved me.

How do we cope, day after day, with glittering anguish, its honed edge? Raveled by inner voices wicked as knives, the promise of youth frays. Diagnosis: paranoid schizophrenia. The shredding begins deep in the fabric of being, and also within those bearing witness.

And now he is gone.

And I am afraid to look deeper.

※ ※ ※

When I try to face Michael's suicide, sadness collides with guilt. Seeking relief, I rationalize. He's at peace now. He need not bear the current global weight of sorrow as death tolls rise—Covid, violence, war, drought, starvation.

Bewilderment strands me, creating a gap that widens beneath my breastbone. Feeling strung between the personal and the eternal, my lungs are a dried riverbed: dust and exposed rock. Breath snags.

I need a haven. So, I sign up for a guided meditation class to be held online. Can *I* be held by others I can't even touch? Feeling threadbare, I ponder the notion of digital mending—figurative, of course.

※ ※ ※

On the day of class, in the virtual Zoom room, Sandra is the hearth radiating warmth. I pull my device closer, discover the Comments feature as fellow participants type in their hopes for our session. We hail from various countries. Seems we are like-minded, longing for comfort, renewal, and wisdom.

Eager to practice mutual quietude, we all agree to be muted.

Yes, it feels artificial. Implausible. We are alone, together. Will we be able to converse? A pandemic-Zoom-newbie, I'm banking on empathy sensed remotely. Already I miss shared, palpable breathing, that singular living stillness I would normally lean on in a support group.

But oh, these eyes of mine feast on smiles, unmasked. Chins, jawlines, teeth are a revelation. Yet this mortal nose hankers after a whiff of hair spray or aftershave. And where is the droll music of bellies primed for lunch?

Above all, I miss touch.

How melodious, then, touchingly so, the voice of our leader, who beckons us onward. In addition to the enlarged view of Sandra, thumbnail headshots animate my screen, my own mug included. *Oh dear. Adjust posture. Tweak the hair. Is it really that limp?*

"I invite you to close your eyes," Sandra says. "Open yourself to whatever might bolster your hope."

*Thicker hair would be nice.* And then: *Why am I making jokes?*

"Now I'd like you to picture yourself receiving a gift, to support you in your spiritual journey."

I want a map. Better yet, a take-me-away magic carpet.

In my mind's eye, an inchworm appears.

Imagination suggests a creature spanning my fingertip, spineless yet plucky, green as the first lettuce leaves in spring. Bemused, I flex my hand. The image persists—so vivid it almost tickles. As if poised for exploring me, moving knuckle to palm, my pretend companion's tiny hind feet initiate micro-steps . . . until *hump*, goes the legless, ungainly middle. Then the front end takes over. It's like watching a relay race with a single entrant. Grinning, I look up.

Everyone's eyes remain closed.

I reenter my bubble, intimate as submersing in water, breath held. Can my virtual gift-worm swim? Can it stitch through the waves like a basting thread? A ripple of affection surprises me. Perhaps it is gauging progress, section by section, using its own body.

I wonder about my nephew. Did he ever pace alongside the river racing headlong through town? He seemed to endure a thought-life no longer tethered. Where the disturbed mind leads, the feet will follow.

His haywire choices laid bare a lie I have embraced: peace is a birthright. Michael, however, persevered through days and nights on the streets, in jail, and in treatment, ever-susceptible to paranoia's hell.

An ache seizes my hip, and I shift positions. My hair clip lands on my knee. *Plip.*

I once heard an inchworm drop from a tree onto the park bench where I sat eating my lunch. Its upper body rose like a periscope, presumably to regain its bearings. Then it swayed, as if dreaming of eventual moth-dom. But how to get there? Its anti-gravity antics embodied a living question mark.

I wonder, are we born into questions already in motion?

Michael has flown now, his lifespan complete. His name derives from the Hebrew word *Mikha'el*, meaning "who is like God?" or "gift from God."

What do I do with that?

Sandra's voice intervenes: "As you consider your gift, do you sense a question or invitation?"

I think of Hans Christian Anderson's inchworm, laboriously crossing the marigolds. Why, he wonders, can't the tired creature simply rest in what *is?* All seems to be a relentless pressing, ever-onward.

Feeling awkward and vulnerable, I yearn to move forward. But I'm lost in a stalemate. No soundtrack. No dialogue. No reprieve from the pulsing silence. Why does one person suffer? Why is another self-paralyzed?

Did Michael forswear wings that day he leapt from the city bridge?

The river answers: I once held a boy who thought he was saving himself.

> *The rivers*
> *have names they repeat forever,*
> *just out of hearing.* —Robert Morgan, "Visitors"

℣ ℣ ℣

Online, Sandra taps her Tibetan singing bowl, calling me back into the present. As the hollow chime hangs in the air, vibrations *zing* in my gums and intricate sinus bones. It makes my eyes water.

"I hope some of you will share," she says.

Electronic comments whiz past like an itemized receipt: laments and small visitations. My vision strains, so I resurrect the gallery view. Two dozen faces fill my screen, twenty-four life stories, side-by-side, 240,000 things that went right so that each person could be born.

The collective gaze seems to hold mine, and the untraveled span between us shrinks. Feeling held, I lean upon a visceral calm.

A bridge should not be a symbol of horror. Trust aligns and allows for crossings.

℣ ℣ ℣

What is this tiny throb? I pause. It feels like a thorn, pricking deep within, as if a very fine needle stitches through tissues that crisscross my heart. Breath slows. I gaze again at my journey mates, faces like maps, their eyes luminous as miniature lanterns.

It's not that I sense the gift-worm leaving my palm, but I feel different. Less alone. Tenderly marked.

Michael, can you hear me? What dazzling patterns are you painting now, tumbleweed boy? What sacred flying leap awaits?

I cradle the question posed by your name: "Who is God?" Perhaps these days both of you pray for me.

## MARK BARKAWITZ

### *TEN YEARS, HUH?*

    I'm comfortably seated in my usual recliner with a prewarmed blanket the nurse has placed over my legs, reading the *L.A. Times* Sports page, while hooked-up to an intravenous drip of methylprednisolone in my forearm.

    At the far end of the clean, white, medical room that I refer to as Dr. Hu's Chemo Lounge, a middle-aged bear of a man—6'5", 6'6", barrel-chested, wearing a plaid flannel with rolled-up sleeves, jeans, and worn Timberlands—enters.

    He chooses a nearby recliner—the rectangular room has a dozen-or-so, sporadically filled with other patients, half of whom are dozing behind the surgical masks we all wear—with the nurses' station on the opposite side.

    I go back to my Sports page.

    When next I look up, the big guy has removed his shirt. Bare to the waist—he exposes the two, clear tubes of a catheter—hanging like a bolo tie—on the left side of his hairy chest just below his throat.

    "That a Hickman?" I ask.

    He looks over, nods.

    "Yeah."

    "I had one of those about ten years ago. Handy device."

    The accommodating ends of the hose-like tubes allow the nurses to screw in drip bags of medicine, completely eliminating the need for needles. I had a stem cell transplant at City of Hope—seventeen days in isolation—and never once got stuck with a needle!

    "Leukemia," he says.

    "Multiple myeloma," I reply.

    Pause.

    "Ten years, huh?"

# STEPHANIE HART

## *ONLY NOW*

It is the early time of Covid. I'm at a writing workshop on Martha's Vineyard in a circle of women in face masks. Seated six feet apart in our instructor's backyard, we are wary of each other. Are there germs in the air that might kill us? Will we pummel each other with criticism?

Our instructor, Sally Henry, is a genteel woman in her late thirties. Dressed in a green peasant blouse and harem paints, she speaks in a serene voice. She welcomes us and invites us to feel comfortable during our time together. We introduce ourselves, talk briefly about the joys of writing: the catharsis of memoir, the delight when fictional characters come to life. And the pitfalls: the times when characters stubbornly refuse to speak, and memoir falls short of the emotional mark we want to reach. Sally listens attentively. She says, "Why not put aside your writing projects for today. We'll pause, breathe, and inhabit the moment as we write through the senses." Her blue eyes are earnest, but I'm perplexed. I'm not fond of meditative practices. I have a restless mind, silence frightens me.

Sally, I think, tries to assuage any doubts we may have with a story from her own life. She tells about her daughter Melissa's chronic illness, how it riddled her with fear, worry. How she could not be present in a way that was comforting to Melissa. Then, daily walks in the woods began to fortify her. Each morning she would hug the thick bark of a tree, let shade and shadow play over her body.

Sally smiles at us with her blue eyes. "I learned to commune with each moment as if there were no other. This pause allowed my body and soul to quiet. In time, I acquired vitality and calm to take to my daughter's bedside."

Sally presses her hands together. "Now we're going to apply this same principle to liberating your creative energy. Giving you freedom from constraint on the page. Are you game?"

We nod. Myself more reluctantly than the other women.

"Okay then. Let's begin. Close your eyes. Now breath in slowly through your nose and out through your mouth. Pause. Clear your mind. Breath in again."

My mind is anything but clear. I want to open my eyes to check for bees in the vicinity, for women who have dropped their masks, releasing Covid particles in the air, for storm clouds that might be gathering. Who will be on danger alert if I'm not?

Sally keeps talking. After a while her voice becomes a chant. One I almost want to listen to. "Pause. Breath in and out. Clear your mind. Now choose a color from the spectrum. Let your color enter from the top of your head and move through your body."

I choose blue for its soothing properties.

"Pause," Sally says. "Breath. Keep your focus on your color and its movement."

Despite my desire to remain vigilant, I feel my body relax. I'm floating on my back on blue sea where waves cradle rather than threaten me. Thoughts slip away without my willing them to.

"Breath in, breath out," Sally says. "One more time. Now slowly open your eyes. Look around you. When you're ready, pick up your pen. Record what you see, hear, feel, and smell. Don't let thoughts bog you down. Write as if you were flying."

I open my eyes. Survey the scenery. Sights, sounds, colors come alive with a vibrancy that is new. I'm experiencing the backyard for the first time. My pen moves easily across the page. This is what I write:

*I feel the wind, I hear chimes, a motor hums, birds sing and stop. I hear a rake, a hammer, and a whistle. I see red, yellow and orange wildflowers. I watch them bend unselfconsciously.*

Something catches the corner of my eye. I turn toward it. I discover rocks on a table and a giant sand-colored five-point star nailed to the gray brick of a New England house. I see white lace curtains on a rectangular window. I see a profusion of blue flowers, fists of delicate petals. I see perfectly clear sky and giant trees, green leaves against the blue, trembling and then still. I see a chimney made (I think) of Flemish brick. There! Was that so difficult?

Attunement to the moment is rare for me, and so now gives me a heady feeling. My writing flourishes in the coming days of the workshop. I capture my grandmother's spirit as she stands on the deck of a ship escaping the Russian pogroms and heading for America. The other women write with a fluency and honesty, which is stunning. At the end of the week, we offer Sally our gratitude. Sally sends us off with praise and more importantly with a challenge. "Take your ability to pause and come back stronger, not only into your creative life but also into daily life."

Once back in New York, this challenge proves to be more difficult than anything I had anticipated. In fact, it becomes the greatest challenge of my life. Covid sears through the nation, killing my cousin, bringing a friend to the brink of death. The stories I read of people in hospitals across the nation, dying alone without family are heart breaking and terrifying. People without the means to leave work to keep out of harm's way.

Sequestered in our apartment, my husband and I resort to name-calling. I tell him he has a mean streak and a wild temper; he tells me I'm rude, and don't give enough to the relationship.

My cancer reasserts itself, this time threatening my life. A prominent doctor at a world-class hospital declares me terminal. I rail about seeking second and third opinions. I'm in a maze of indecision. Will visualizing a blue light really save me from a morass of terror and confusion? My natural skepticism causes me to doubt it. However, trying to tackle my problems head on only seems to exacerbate them. I'm in the woods with no tree to hold onto.

I decide to extend my visualization process. Reading, listening to tapes, and watching YouTube videos gives me a framework from which to develop my own practice. First, I begin by relaxing every part of my body: eyes, forehead, throat chest, stomach legs and feet. I notice a tendency to hold my breath. As Sally taught us, I breath in slowly and deeply and then out again. I pause. I close my eyes. Then choose a color from the spectrum. Blue again. Sometimes yellow for energy. I find myself floating on a cloud touched by gentle sunlight. I picture the cancer in my pelvis being carried away by currents of blue and yellow light. In another exercise, I stand under a shimmering white and gray waterfall and invite anyone who I've had conflict with to join me. We bath in a shower of mutual forgiveness. The weight of resentment is one I don't miss.

As weeks pass, I become calmer, less fearful. I find a new oncologist who promotes healing in my body. Perhaps I'm helping him along. I try and sometimes succeed in taking one moment at a time. I have not acquired the equanimity of the Dalai Lama. Anger and angst rear their heads. Anger at cancer, at my husband, and at myself for not being stronger, more disciplined.

I find out negative thought patterns are inordinately difficult to break, forces to be reckoned with. Yet, as the chemotherapy drips through my veins, I'm able to focus on the delights in Sally Henry's backyard: a profusion of blue flowers, trembling green leaves, vibrant colored tulips. I pause. I breathe in and out, garnering the courage to face what I have to face.

On the days when I can quell nausea and fatigue, my writing takes on power. Dialogue is less stilted, the action sharper. My narrative characters describe scenes in their own idiom. Finally, I'm bringing them to life.

In my daily life, my power of observation has become keener and more instinctual. From my eleventh story window, I watch sunsets and cloud formations, the moon waxing and waning in a navy sky. Tonight, my husband points out a line of billowing pink clouds etched in blue lines among the buildings, coating the sky at dusk. We hold hands in wonder, totally absorbed in the moment.

## ANNA STEEGMANN

*IN A SILENT WAY*

Sitting by myself,
letting it sink in,
Myelodysplastic Syndromes, my diagnosis.

Sitting on a bench
in Central Park's Conservatory Garden,
a block from the doctor's office
where I received the devastating news.

Comforted by the birds, the trees, the plants.
They will still be here
when I'm gone, when I'm gone.

The only possible cure for MDS
is a bone marrow transplant,
the doctor said. We start you on chemo first.

I'm not ready.
I want to sit here
in silence as long as I can.

# ARLENE GAY LEVINE

## *THE WAITING ROOM*

Dermatologist's office. Tuesday morning. 11:30 a.m.
Soft classical music. Chopin, I think. Hard wood chairs.
Every seat is filled but one. I take my place, dreading the wait.
The other patients are elderly, their feathery white caps
a contrast to my bark brown hair now copper-streaked
with henna to hide the first gray strands.
A late October light shines through their skin giving
it the appearance of golden Depression era glass.
The frailest woman wears large gauze bandages
on her face and arms. When she catches me observing
she flashes the most loving of smiles. My tense face
relaxes and I return the kindness, eyes shining
warmth for a fragile stranger.
Why am I smiling,
I think a moment later, here to investigate
a minute freckle, a recently arrived gray dot
that henna will not help.

The young doctor enters the waiting room, calls a name.
No one moves. She calls again and we patients set to looking
at each other, wondering whose turn it is, and why they don't go.
I sense it is this sparrow of a woman the doctor wants; I turn toward her,
repeat the name. Yes, her tiny head bobs. Slowly, she rises
and wobbles her way into the inner office.
I don't see her again. When my turn comes, I disappear too.
"It may be benign, possibly not," the doctor says. "The only way
to be sure is to remove it. There will be a scar."

I decide to watch and wait, the other option she offers,
"not without some risk" as if to emphasize her disapproval of my choice.
When I leave, I am amazed to feel relief though nothing's been settled.
I feel light, almost translucent, like the skin of the old ones, happy
with my new willingness to wait. Stepping into the unknown,
life seems so suddenly full
of possibilities.

## THE ART OF FIRE MAKING

There is nothing worse than someone who throws water
on your fire or urges you to build one when for reasons
of your own, right then, you haven't the heart for it.

Fire making is an inside job; it begins and ends there.
People can tell you everything about it:
how to start, why, what tools to use
except until you choose to begin
and do it, for yourself, by yourself,
in your own way, the rest is just talk.

Maybe later, after you've made many fires,
understand how hard it is to get the flint
to ignite against rock, fail often
to elicit even a spark, felt the elation when
fanning brought to life a grand roar
of red and gold, maybe some
of what they told you will make sense.

And maybe not because by then
you will know that talking about making fires
sucks the energy from wood gathering, arranging,
rubbing sticks over and over until friction
becomes the sweet smell of smoke sending
signals to your brain that something's started here.

So listen, but mostly to your own voice,
the one that has all the answers
to all the questions but just needs
time, space and silence
to one day create that fire
only you can
build.

# PATTY SOMLO

## *RAISINS*

I knew the two soft pillows placed in my right palm were raisins. Yet I forced myself to pretend I didn't have a clue what they might be. That was the point, after all, to pretend we were aliens from another planet. With my eyes closed, I tried to figure out for what purpose these squishy blobs might have been created.

Using my left hand, I pressed the larger one down flat, then rolled it into a ball. As if attempting to describe its distinctive characteristics in writing, I let my imagination guide me. Fighting against what I knew, that these were dark, plump raisins, I told myself a lie. *This is dough*, I said silently, as I rolled and flattened, rolled and flattened. *I will use this to make two miniature pizzas.*

Sitting in a hard, straight-backed chair, my feet planted firmly on the floor, I was in my first class on mindfulness meditation. The exercise aimed to impart an aspect of mindfulness, that of beginner's mind. We were exploring the difference between knowing, or at least thinking we knew, and letting the world teach us through feel, texture and smell, as it did when we were young.

The majority of the thirty or so students in the room were far from young. Nearly everyone, including me, fell comfortably in the Boomer years. I couldn't be sure if my generation predominated because we had long been attracted to Eastern practices and thought, or if this was due to the fact that cancer tends to affect more people at this stage of life. The class had been offered by a local hospital's cancer support center. All of the students were either cancer patients or family members. Except for two women who'd gone bald, it was impossible to tell which students were patients and which were not.

At the beginning of the class, Annie, the instructor, had said that when we meditated, unpleasant emotions might come up. I knew this already, having spent more than half a dozen years in therapy, based on an Integrative Psychology model that combined Western talk therapy with meditation.

For years, I began each fifty-minute session sitting across from my therapist, Laura, with my feet flat on the floor, eyes closed, watching the breath as it traveled in through my nostrils, into my lungs, and down, all the way to my feet. Watching the breath enabled me to feel, something I'd cleverly managed to avoid for years.

On this morning, in a large room with plain brown wooden cabinets running the length of the east wall, Annie led us in our first meditation. All she wanted us to do was watch the breath, coming in and going out. Each time the mind jumped away from the breath, we were advised to gently bring it back, maybe even labeling it with words, such as *planning* or *thinking*.

I had barely closed my eyes and focused on my breath when I realized how sad I felt. The sorrow crowded around my temples, pressing against my eyes. I knew I was supposed to bring my thoughts back to the breath, but all I could think about was how badly I wanted to cry.

The sadness was suddenly washed away by a stab of anger I couldn't ignore. And what made me angrier was that I couldn't take my fury out on anyone, because there was no one to blame.

I was angry that my husband, Richard, had gotten cancer. Even more infuriating, he'd been diagnosed when the cancer had spread to his bones and was no longer curable. He had Stage Four, the worst, most deadly. I was angry because I knew he would one day leave me, something I wasn't the least bit prepared for.

Having always been a person who didn't enjoy following rules, I continued to ignore Annie's reminders to bring my thoughts back to the breath. Instead, I wallowed in that anger, dissecting it, considering each aspect, as I began to understand that there were many. I was furious, I could see now, with *them,* an unnamed group who seemed to control the universe, giving some folks all the luck and others, like Richard and me, most of the heartache. This cancer diagnosis was patently unfair. Anyone could see that. Richard was a kind, thoughtful person. I felt certain that our friends and acquaintances liked him much better than they liked me. He should not have had to suffer like this.

And I went on, listing more of the reasons cancer should not have been allowed to barge into our lives, relenting every fourth or fifth thought to haul my mind back ever so momentarily to the breath. Richard and I had married late, having spent decades finding one another. We had happily imagined growing old and frail together, still laughing a lot, and still getting irritated at each other's most annoying habits.

I had signed up for the mindfulness class as a way to cope. Though I'd long understood that there were absolutely no guarantees in life and this moment was all we had, my mind operated in a dramatically different fashion. For much of my life, I struggled with both anxiety and depression. To cope, I became adept at trying to catapult myself out of the present moment to some imaginary future where things would be just fine.

In a deep way I understood that dwelling on the cancer was not going to help me or Richard. Yes, we needed to pay attention, to understand what treatments were available and how to deal with side effects and maximize his potential for healing. But beyond that, thinking about this disease only seemed to lead down a dark, narrow tunnel without even the thinnest ray of light.

Each time Annie tapped the small bell, the signal to open our eyes, I again became aware of the other people in that room. In one way or another, we were all in the same boat, drifting toward a future none of us could imagine. Yet no one appeared dejected. In fact, when describing their experiences meditating or trying to pretend that a raisin wasn't a raisin, many of the women and men joked.

I quit going to those weekly fifty-minute therapy sessions nearly two decades ago, when I felt I'd said everything to my therapist there was to say. I hadn't been *cured* of depression, as I'd once hoped, but I had learned something profound. I could live with depression. Acknowledgment and acceptance of the depression was at the core. That meant letting in bad feelings, instead of trying to push them away, as I'd done most of my life.

Or as I liked to think, acceptance began with *feeling my feet.* Times when my mood turned dark, I would straighten my back and plant my feet firmly on the floor. My eyes closed, I would watch the breath, as it leaked into my nostrils and down my throat, filling the lungs, then swirling around the belly, before dropping into my thighs and calves, and finally down to my feet. Once the breath was there, I would feel my feet, the big toe and the pinky, the arch, and then up to the ankle. At that point, I often had a clue what moments before had made me feel bad.

The final time Annie had us meditate I fought to keep even the most minute focus on my breath. I felt as if an annoying fly kept landing on me, close to my right eye, and I repeatedly needed to swat it away. At one point, I questioned whether this practice would ever make me feel the slightest bit better. It seemed to be making me feel worse.

A voice in my head was kind enough to remind me that habits are hard to break. And though I wasn't supposed to let my mind sail off into thought, I did so anyway.

For as far back as I could remember, I planned, schemed and daydreamed my way out of unhappy times. The thinking went, *When I go on vacation, then I will be happy,* or *When I get a new job, things will be better.* Yet nearly every time I arrived in that new and different place, I found that nothing had changed.

I couldn't wish, plan or daydream my way out of the current situation, I reminded myself. All I could do was learn to look at the world with a beginner's mind, to take in its beauty, along with the pain. And thinking this, I dragged my mind back, gently trying to focus on the breath, for as long as my attention might deign to stay.

## PAUL HOSTOVSKY

### *THE AIR BETWEEN*

"Can we not talk
for a little bit?"
you said because
you weren't feeling well
and I was trying
to make you feel better
by taking you out
for coffee and doing
most of the talking,
going on and on about
coffee here versus
coffee there, and this
and that—anything, really,
that I could think of
to talk about outside of
your illness, which was
in your body and in
the air between us.
And then I said, "Yes,
of course, sorry."
And you said,
"Thank you."

## *QUITS*

Let's call it quits, let's take
five, no, seven, in honor of
the seventh day. No, in honor
of the cigarette, which takes
exactly seven minutes to smoke
all the way down. Let's take
a break. Let's take a liquid lunch
and not come back for days,
weeks, months. Let's not and say
we did. I used to say that
a lot as a kid: *Let's not and say
we did.* It sounded anarchic
and subversive. I was big into
subversion and anarchy. I quit
high school and landed on my feet
in a college for creative fuck-ups
on the Hudson. I quit marriages
and landed on my feet in other
marriages. I'm all for quitting.
Quitting gets a bad rap. The people
who tell you to never give up—
to keep fighting no matter what—
don't you just want to slap them?
A few of them are standing around
my hospital bed right now, telling me
to keep fighting. I want to get up
and slap them, one by one, then
hug them, hard, and say I love you,
then lie back down and call it quits.

## *MALINGERING*

Something irresistibly sweet
about being sick. Beyond
the getting a pass, the being excused
from school, from work,
from life, actually. Something
about life and death and lying down
in the place where they meet:
the sickbed, that approximately-equal-to sign
with a squiggly mark on top
like a rumpled sheet or blanket,
so inviting, so irresistible,
so sweet. Come back to bed, it says. Climb in
and lie down here in the middle
of the equation: two expressions
of approximately equal value: life
on the one side, death on the other. In this warm
bed (you are very warm, where
is the thermometer?) you can really stretch out.
Go ahead, stretch your arms
over your head and you can almost touch
life itself somewhere just beyond
your head. Stretch your ten
poor stubby toes and you can almost feel
death down there just below your feet—what a sweet
tease. Tickle, tickle.

## THE HURT ITSELF

There was no one to blame
when I closed the laptop
and got up from the chair
and tripped over the cat

(who was just sitting there
quietly minding his own
ruminations in the shadow
of the chair) and fell forward

and hit my shoulder hard
against the fireplace mantle,
jamming my index finger,
and knocking over a knick-knack

made of glass (which belonged
to my mother, who'd been dead
twenty-nine years). I winced
and held my aching shoulder,

and licked my smarting knuckle,
and surveyed the broken glass.
And then I looked around for
someone to blame. It wasn't

my fault that I didn't see the cat
hidden in the shadow. It wasn't
the cat's fault for being a cat
ruminating in shadow behind a chair,

and it wasn't my mother's fault
for buying a glass knick-knack,
and dying, and leaving it to me.
Leave it to me, I always find

someone to blame. But this time
there was no one, there was nothing.
Which hurt more than the hurt itself
almost. And then it hurt differently

than the hurt. Then less than the hurt.
And finally, in that pause, not blaming
anyone for the hurt itself didn't hurt at all.
And it felt new. It felt good. Almost.

# III
# TRAUMA

# BETH CHRISTENSEN

## *TWENTY-FIVE YEARS*

1974

I am just shy of seventeen years old, beginning my senior year at a small Catholic high school in a run-down section of town, the kind of place from which white people are fleeing to the suburbs and the buildings themselves seem to be throwing in the towel. High school has been difficult for me and is getting more so all the time. I hate my teachers, my classes, and all but a couple of my classmates. I don't study—I *can't* study—anymore, so my grades suck. My thinking has become increasingly fragmented and confusing, like a bunch of Scrabble pieces spilled onto the floor. There is often yelling going on inside my head, voices that I know but don't know. I get yelled at by other people, too—parents and teachers mostly. When they yell at me, I often have trouble understanding what they are saying. I wish it would all just quiet down, just for a little while. Pot makes it quiet down, or at least it makes me less bothered by all the noise. At this point I am smoking a lot of pot.

I go to a psychiatrist once a week. I have been seeing him for about two years and taking the medications he has prescribed for me, but I haven't been getting any better; in fact, I have been getting worse and by now am quite sure that I am becoming insane. His office is a short bus ride from my school. I get on the bus near school, and it sighs and heaves its way down a narrow street past old, mostly neglected mansions, shotgun houses with tattered shutters on their windows and faded peeling paint, and narrow, dingy storefronts the dozen or so blocks to my stop. I get off the bus, and as I walk the three blocks to my doctor's office my head gets lighter, feeling kind of like a helium balloon on a string, and it feels as if, were I to let go of the string, it might disappear altogether—kind of like the feeling you get when you are about to faint, but I don't faint. I open the iron gate with a rusty hinge that creaks with a tortured moan, and I walk up to the door of this old Victorian house that has been carved up into offices. I know my legs are carrying me, but I can't really feel them anymore. I seem to float up the dark wooden stairs; they creak with every step, and the fact that I am able to produce a sound is somewhat surprising to me.

At the top of the stairs there is a receptionist tucked into a tiny office. She answers phone calls and types, making what seem to me to be efficient clacking sounds, and I just step into the doorway of her little office. I don't have to tell her my name, she already knows who I am. She says something to me, or maybe she just nods in recognition of my arrival, and I take a seat in his narrow waiting room. My floating head and absent legs are still there, but now I become more aware of the pounding of my heart. I wonder if someone could see it beating through my shirt, the feeling of it beating is so strong. My hands are clammy, and I wipe them repeatedly on my blue plaid school skirt, pressing it against my thighs. I want to run away, but I can't. I don't know why I can't, but I can't. This question would torture me many years later: Why didn't I just run away? Surely I could have gotten up and left, so why didn't I? Why? It would become one of the hardest questions I would ever have to confront.

His door opens, and I hear his voice. That voice is imprinted on my mind, so strongly that if I heard him in a crowd of a thousand people, I could pick out his voice and my heart would pound again. His patient, the one he has just finished seeing, is going down the creaking stairs now, and then I hear him close the door at the bottom of the stairway. The doctor says good night to his receptionist, and I hear her gathering her things before she too heads down the resonant stairs and out of the building. I'm his last appointment of the day. The building is quiet, and I feel him stepping into the waiting room before I see him. His voice—that voice that is like no other—speaks my name and I obediently stand up and follow him into his office. He closes his doors; there are two of them with a space between them, and each one locks. He says that the double doors are for privacy, so people in the hallways or the waiting room can't hear what we are saying. I already know that there is no one who will hear me, regardless of the doors. I now belong fully to him, and he leads my automaton-like body through the main room, furnished with a sofa and chairs, into the second room, which is outfitted only with large floor pillows over a thick reddish carpet. He had told me once that this room was used for group therapy. He looks at me and smiles as he says something, but I don't know what he is saying. Whatever it is, as he says it, he is beginning to unbutton my shirt and his breathing gets hard, hungry like a big bad wolf in a cartoon. I slip into a state of even more disconnection from my body as he undresses me and then himself, and then his hands are on me, and he guides my hands and my mouth on him, and then he is in me.

I'm not sure exactly when this—the sex—started. The first time I saw him, it was the summer before my sophomore year, when I was fourteen years old. I thought he was remarkably cool for an old guy. He would sit across from me in his big leather chair, puffing on a pipe, looking at me with these really intense eyes. He had eyes that seemed to be able to see right through me, that seemed capable of popping right out of his head and attaching themselves to me, like leeches. He would let me smoke cigarettes, and he would ask me about myself, about school and friends and my family, and when I answered he seemed to really listen. I was starving for that kind of validation, and I'm sure he knew it.

Eventually he started asking if he could hug me at the end of our sessions. I said OK. I had no idea whether this was normal, and at that point I didn't want to do anything to push away this man who I thought was one of the very few people, and the only adult, who really got me. At some point, the hugs got tighter and longer, and I could feel his erection against me. I didn't know what to do about that. I think that at some point I tried shortening the hugs, but I don't think I succeeded. It wasn't long after that, that the hugs turned to deep kisses, and the kisses into sex. I was, I think, fifteen years old when that started, and every week we would go into his "group" room, with the red carpet and the floor pillows, and he would undress me as if I were a doll on Christmas morning. I felt just as unreal as one.

I was, to be sure, a troubled kid when I started seeing him. Experiences in my early life had left me angry and rebellious, and a deep rage had been building in me for years that I did not understand. When I got to high school, it was as if the brakes were released, and I went careening down into drugs and all kinds of acting-out. This doctor was known to my family. He was considered to be kind and caring, as I understand it, and my mother liked and trusted him, and so he became my psychiatrist.

I kept getting worse. I don't know if or to what extent, at the time, I was really aware of the sexual abuse that was going on in session. I think that, while it was happening, I often was able to leave my body to some degree—not floating near the ceiling like some people describe, but able to disconnect my consciousness from the physical and emotional reality of what was happening. As time went on, I got quite good at this kind of dissociation. I got so good at it that I could cut long, angry red gashes into my arms and legs without feeling any pain. I could do risky things, like driving recklessly or walking through dangerous neighborhoods to score drugs, and I didn't feel scared; in fact, I felt more alive when I was tempting death. It wasn't that I didn't think I might get hurt or die; I felt like I was already dead. Dealing loose joints behind the gym at school, I never worried about getting busted. What could they do? Put me in jail? That was OK, I would probably get raped less often in there. Fear in general, like pain, was something I had learned to not feel. So on it went, until the fall of my senior year.

One day, I think it was in November, something happened at school. I had my knife out, the same one I used to cut myself, but I was threatening someone else—a teacher maybe? I don't know how they found out that I had a shrink—I guess they called my mother—but he apparently arranged for me to go directly into the psychiatric hospital. I was terrified and enraged, and then I think I just went blank for a while. I remember waking up in a cold, kind of dark room. I was in a bed with leather straps around my wrists and ankles and one around my waist, and all of them were connected to the bed so I couldn't move. I tried to call for help, but I couldn't locate my voice at first. Eventually a woman came in, who turned out to be an aide of some sort. She was no more than five feet tall and a bit beyond plump. She spoke in a voice that was at once soothing and authoritative. I told her I needed to get up, I needed to pee. She said I had to wait until my doctor arrived to give her orders to unshackle me. I eventually peed in the bed, and by the time the doctor came my pee had turned cold.

At first the doctor scolded me, like a misbehaving child, for what I had done. I guess he was upset about the knife, not the pee. But who knows? He kept me in the hospital, but out of the restraints, for a few days, then released me. I went back to school where everyone knew I had been sent away somewhere, and I heard the murmurs follow me like a wake, and felt the stares burning my back as I walked away. I think that was the first time that I realized that there was nowhere I wanted to be. Not at school, not at home, not at the hospital. But I kept going to his office every week, and he kept raping me. Before long, I was back in the hospital.

In January or February of senior year, as he continued to rape me (at least once while I was actually in the hospital), my dissociation became complete. I left my body and was unable to return to it. He told my family that I was catatonic, and for about two weeks I was unable to move, to speak, to eat or drink. There was some concern, I found out later, that I might die. I remember some of the process of trying to come out of it—it was like being under deep, dark water, trying to come to the surface but being kept down by the weight of the water. I remember hearing my mother talking to me, trying to elicit a response from me, and it sounded like she was so far away. After a while—weeks, I suppose—I was able to get up but only with monumental effort, as if my blood had been drained and replaced with lead. Speaking was difficult as well; if someone asked me a question, by the time I was able to formulate and articulate even a simple answer, the person would likely have moved on. The hospital people kept scolding me, telling me that I needed to go to group therapy or art therapy or whatever, and all I could do was to look at them as the idiots they were. How could I do art therapy with lead-filled arms?

At some point, he declared me schizophrenic, and thus began years of off-and-on institutionalization, countless doses of Thorazine and other powerful drugs, and dozens of electroshock treatments. I realize now that the diagnosis of schizophrenia and the drugs and the shock treatments had a particular benefit for the doctor: They probably helped me forget what he had done to me, and even if I did remember and muster the courage to tell anyone, who would believe me? According to my well-respected psychiatrist, I was a delusional psychotic who saw him (and I swear he wrote this, I saw it on my chart years later) as an "unfilled oedipal object." If you're not familiar with Freud, look it up. It's a hoot. At that point, in those years after my first hospitalization, it appeared that this would be my life, for the rest of my life.

## 1999

It is early spring, and I am on my way home from a business trip, feeling good about the contract I had just signed with a tiny hospital in a small Florida panhandle town. I teach critical-care nurses, and I am going to be working with this hospital as they develop more comprehensive services for cardiac patients in their emergency department. This is my first gig as an independent educator/consultant and I'm pretty proud of myself. The drive home is long and takes me close to one of my favorite beaches along the Gulf of Mexico. I stop for the night at a beachfront hotel. I take a walk on the beach, enjoying the cool March breeze and splendid sunset, then I go to my room, order room service, and work on a proposal for another potential job with someone I will be meeting the next day. It is about 11 p.m. when I go to bed.

I have been asleep for maybe an hour when suddenly I bolt out of bed in a panic. For the first time in twenty-five years, I remember what the doctor did. I remember the sex and feelings of craziness and unreality, and somehow I know without a doubt that what I remember now is real and true. This happened, I am absolutely sure of it (this would later be confirmed by the doctor himself). I don't understand how I could have been unaware of it for twenty-five years. The memories are mental, but they are also physical. They crush my chest and stab me, deep, between my legs. I smell his pipe smoke and I hear his deep gravelly voice. More than anything, I see his hungry eyes. I feel them boring into me, and I know that they are looking at me, looking all the way through me, just like they always did. I feel terrified, suffocating. I open the sliding door and step onto the balcony of my hotel room. I hear the waves breaking softly on the shore, and I feel the damp salt breeze on my skin, but I can't breathe—I go out to the edge of the balcony, grabbing the railing, gulping as much air as I can, but I still feel as if I am suffocating. God, where is the air? Why can't I breathe?

The memories keep coming, crashing into me like waves, like the sickening waves that rock a boat on a stifling hot day. My terror and confusion in this moment are exactly like the terror and confusion I am beginning to remember. Why did he do this to me? How could he have done this to me? And what did it all mean? The memories, the sensations, and the questions bounce around in my mind for the rest of the night. When it is morning, I pack up my things. I am thinking of canceling my meeting, but I don't. I have been wanting to work with this person for a long time, and I am still somehow believing that my life belongs to me. So, I drive the hour and a half to her office, and I manage to get through the meeting. We agree to work on a small project together.

Back in the car and on the road, I finally start to fully absorb what is happening, and I drive the remaining two hours home crying and trying to make sense out of everything I am thinking and feeling. I remember the feeling of things being distant and unreal, of my experiences seeming crazy, and I begin to realize that so much of the horror of my life at that time, horror that had been explained by this doctor as symptoms of schizophrenia, was because of what he had done to me. This realization is overwhelming in what it meant back then, and in what it means now. My head is racing with the rush of memories and with the sharp, piercing understanding of what this all means. My life had been a lie. It would be a while before I would be able to call what he did to me "rape," or to understand my reaction as severe post-traumatic stress and dissociation, but even in those first days and weeks of remembering, I knew that he had hurt me terribly. What I didn't know, what I could not have imagined, was how hard it would be to heal, and how profoundly my life and, indeed, my very self would change.

2022

I have done mountains of therapy work on the sexual abuse, the psychiatric abuse, the process of remembering, and the costs of all those elements on my life, my family, my careers, and my health. But until now I had never considered, at least to the extent that it deserves, the nature or purpose of the twenty-five-year pause in my awareness. Call it recovered memories, repression, dissociative amnesia—call it whatever you like, but for some reason, some *good* reason, I lost awareness of what he had done to me.

After the catatonic-type condition, the slow struggle to return to the world of the living, and the two or so years of hospitals, drugs, and electroshocks, I began to get better. He turned my care over to another doctor, and later I moved far away from my rapist and everything that represented him. I brought safe, healthy people into my life. I began, slowly at first, to believe that my life might have some value. I realize that twenty-five years is pretty long as pauses go, but a lot of important things happened in those years.

I went to college and discovered, to my great surprise, that I was smart—smart enough to graduate summa cum laude with a bachelor's degree in nursing. I started working in intensive care, earned specialty certification, and held several offices in the local chapter of my specialty nursing organization.

I got married. I started graduate school. I had my first child between semesters, then finished my master's degree in nursing. I taught pathophysiology to baccalaureate nursing students. I lectured at conferences on the local, regional, and national level. I got published in a peer-reviewed journal, which was released just a few weeks before my twins were born. I wrote my first textbook chapter, often with one of them on each knee.

My husband and I created a happy, healthy family. We went hiking and camping and took long car trips. We went to museums and libraries and science fairs and picnics. We both loved being parents. Our children were smart and creative, talented and funny. I spent many evenings and Saturdays in the bleachers at local playgrounds, cheering on whoever was playing whatever sport that day, or at the school theater, trying to fit a too-small child into a too-large costume. And I continued to advance professionally, until finally I took that leap and began my education and consulting practice. But, for reasons I could not yet understand, I never felt good enough, smart enough, talented enough. I couldn't quantify that standard of *enough*, but I knew I could never reach it. I was always waiting for my life to fall apart, for the schizophrenia to come out of remission and ruin me.

For a long time, I hated thinking about that twenty-five-year interval of apparent normalcy and accomplishment because it was so painful to realize how much I had lost, and to think of what might have been. Might I have gone to medical school, as I had long ago wanted to do, but thought that my history of schizophrenia would preclude? Could I have traveled, or might I have had some success as a writer or an artist? But when I look at it now, as a pause, I realize that those years were when I developed the strength I would later need to recover from the remembering, the re-living, the process of making sense out of the hell that I had been through. Had I not had the benefit of that pause, I think I would have died. Just as my catatonia had brought me to the edge of death, my loss of memory led me away from that edge and allowed me to live.

I knew that I needed to make some meaning out of my experiences, both the abuse and the long, painful—sometimes excruciating—process of healing. As I progressed in my recovery, I realized that I had learned a lot about healing, and that I might be able to put that knowledge to good use, to create meaning out of something that otherwise had none. I earned a master's then a doctorate in mental health counseling.

The clients I work with now have not had a pause; they have maintained conscious awareness of their abuse since its beginning. But for a couple of them at least, I wish that they could have had the benefit of a pause. Smart, talented women, they carry within themselves the severely wounded child they once were, and that child has not been given the chance to learn to hope and to trust, to learn that love doesn't have to be dangerous, and that they are capable of so much more than they believe they are. Yes, twenty-five years is a long time for a pause. But as I look back on it now, I think it was exactly the amount of time I needed, and I am grateful for it.

## EDWARD A. DOUGHERTY

*FIT FOR HEAVEN*

—i—
It was Christmas.
I remember that.

All I ever wanted
was peace, not some
crappy harp-and-
angel peace,

just a kitchen
without screaming,
bedroom walls
that didn't thump.

I spent lots of time
in that dark closet.

—ii—
It was Christmas, and I got her a bracelet,
saved up since Labor Day, even got overtime.

They gave me a coin, first at thirty days,
then sixty, then ninety. I thought I'd beat it.

It was Christmas, and the snow—
I can't blame clouds and cold.

I can't blame all those damn Santas or tinsel.
But it was Christmas, I know that.

—iii—
That cabin was nice,
best place I ever lived.
As an adult anyway.

I prided myself
on being able to sleep
anywhere—cardboard

under a bridge? You bet.
Abandoned hut
in the woods,

no heat? Hell, yeah.
Firetrap of a building
in Baltimore? No problem.

Not her, though.
She's the one
who got me hoping.

—iv—
From what the cops and firemen told me
I sounded just like dear old Dad, ranting
and kicking shit all over the yard
even as the fire lit up the whole neighborhood.

I remember people's faces in the street,
cheeks aglow and eyes glinting back
reflected flames. Their eyes were so wide.
Watching the house burn, watching a madman

ranting about *his woman*, about *his* Christmas tree.
Watching her slam the door and back out
and drive away. Through the window, her face
looked so wet. Yeah, I remember that, too.

—v—

They showed me
the bracelet—
crusty with soot,
chain kinked
out of roundness.

I didn't deserve
to give her
anything
that nice.
And I didn't.

When I got out
I gave back
all my coins.
Now Christmas
is day one.

# KEVIN BROWN

## *SAVING THE MUSIC*

"Pause the tape just right, just a second before the plane hits," Jeff says, staring at the screen, "and think of all those people you save." Taking a shot of bourbon, it dribbling down his chin, the front of his shirt, he says, "Freeze it just right, you still got the towers."

He pours another shot and his hand shakes the bottle into a blur, sloshing liquor on the floor. Everything he says echoes through the empty house. Bounces off bare walls. His wife, Pam, took everything. The couches and tables, beds and dressers. Their daughter's toys and clothes. All that's left are ruts in the hardwood floors and imprints in the carpet. Sheetrock with nail holes like bullet wounds. A couple lawn chairs, his mini-TV. The Mickey Mouse VCR.

And the tape.

I finger-nail the label off a sweating beer. I turn it in my hand and look at the ceiling, at the window, the stairs and door. Anything to keep from looking at what's happening on the screen. What's about to happen, about to start everything that ends with us sitting in this gutted house, I've already seen. Live and unedited. And I don't want to see it again.

"Stop the Zapruder tape at frame 207," he says, "history's rewritten."

"Why you doing this to yourself?" I say.

Not breaking his trance on the screen, he says, "Take his brother. Freeze him at the podium, and he's not gunned down in that kitchen." Downing the shot, he says, "He'd always be 'On to Chicago.'"

My eyes cut to the television, then away. Back to the television.

On it, framed in the 14" x 21" screen, is a shaking mini birthday party. There's a mini clown in the background twisting red balloons into a tiny poodle. There's kids zipping by in front of the camera with party hats cocked to the side. Adults in lawn chairs, the same we're sitting in now, relaxing in the shade of a cypress, legs hooked over their knees, waving. A picnic table lined with paper plates and plastic forks and presents leaning-towered at the end.

Everything formatted to fit your screen.

The cameraman's voice says: *Alright, guys.* The camera shimmies and the voice says: *We ready for cake and ice cream?*

Jeff's voice.

The screen says: 01:41:13.

And these scaled-down kids swarm together like feeding fish, wild and high-pitched. Parents step behind their sons and daughters, their knees or elbows or half-faces the only thing visible. My hands reach from out of frame and rub my son Kaden's head.

Pam comes on screen holding a large Hello Kitty cake, seven candles flickering. She sets it in front of their daughter, Dawn, and everyone sings "Happy Birthday." Jeff's voice loudest next to the camera mic.

The song ends and she closes her eyes. Leans over, hooking the dark curls behind her ears. Her cheeks inflate and she blows the candles out, smoke mouse-tailing in the air.

Everyone cheers.

The screen says: 01:47:05.

Taking a drink, his voice gritty, Jeff says, "There's that tightrope walker." He shakes his head, smiles at the screen. "Hit the button while he's still on the wire, he doesn't drop hundreds of feet seconds later." He says, "He stays up there forever."

I lean forward, drape my wrists over my knees, and say, "He still drops, just not again."

On the TV, Jeff's voice says: *Sorry baby.* Says: *We didn't get you anything this year.*

And Dawn cocks her hips to the side, hand on her waist. Hair blowing across her forehead, she smiles and wags her finger.

*Daddy Daddy Daddy,* she says. *You're so silly.*

Jeff rewinds the tape, her finger wagging in quick-reverse. Her hips straighten, hand coming off her waist. He hits play and she does it all again.

*Daddy Daddy Daddy,* she says, and blinking at the screen, Jeff says with her, "You're *so* silly."

The screen says: 01:54:26.

I stand, throw my head back, and let the beer bubble against my lips. Stepping behind him, my footsteps hollow on the floor, I put my hand on his shoulder. "I'm just saying," I say, "video doesn't stop something from happening." I squat beside him, stare at the side of his face, and say, "It's just proof that it *did* happen."

On screen, Dawn's peeling back pink wrapping paper. Ripping it high above her head and letting it drop behind her. Then, her eyes go wide, her mouth wider. Pam claps and says: *Looky there!*

And Jeff's voice says: *What is it?*

*Tickle Me Elmo,* Dawn says, tugging at the box flaps.

She tears open a Dora doll. She digs into an E-Z Bake Oven.

A Justin Bieber Sing-Along Mic.

A Mickey Mouse VCR.

And she keeps digging until the tower of gifts is gone.

Then, Jeff's voice says: *One more!*

Dawn looks around, a finger to her lips.

*Hon,* Jeff's voice says. *What's it Mom's got there?* His finger stretches out in front of the camera, pointing toward the house. And Pam steps from around the corner, pushing a Hello Kitty Big Wheel. A large red bow tied across the handlebars.

All the kids' mouths are dark pits in their faces. My son looks up at me and I squat down and smile. Massage his shoulders before we disappear out of frame, the camera jumping to follow Dawn running toward the toy, screaming. Arms V'd out.

The screen says: 02:00:05.

Jeff's knee pistons in bursts. He sits straight, then leans forward again, elbows on quads. Pours another drink, shoots it, and pours another.

I grab a beer from the box. Water drips into pucker marks on the floor. "What's say we get out of here," I tell him. "Get something to eat."

His knee moving faster, it vibrates up his torso, bounces his shoulder and head. He says, "That treasurer in Pennsylvania? The one that blew the back of his head out on live TV?" He thumb-rubs the Mickey Mouse-eared remote in his hand and says, "One click of a button, he lives forever." He smiles at his daughter laughing on screen and says, "Course the gun'll always be in his mouth, but nothing's without sacrifice."

I shake my head, stare at the screen, and take a sip. What was my wife is not in the video. She's not at the party. Not at our house. Where she's at is in some other family's videos. Smiling and waving into the camera at some other kid's birthday party. "Jeff," I say. "This acting this way, look what all it's cost." I look around at the nothing in the house and say, "*Look!*" and my voice slaps off all the bare spaces and repeats: *Look!*

He doesn't break his trance.

On the screen, Dawn walks toward the camera with the giant bow in both hands. She brings it closer to the lens, closer to the lens, until the screen shakes and goes dark. Until only bits of the party are seen through the loops of ribbon.

Over the dark, the screen says: 02:03:50.

"Video," Jeff says, "is the modern crystal ball." He says, "It's our prophets, our fortune tellers. It lets us see what's gonna happen." He chokes the bottle of liquor and takes a drink. It spills over the corners of his mouth in a frown.

"It doesn't let us see what's gonna happen," I tell him. "It shows us what already did." Taking a sip of beer, I say, "You see the future, but it's in the past."

Jeff smiles, takes a drink, and shakes his head. "The camera's our fountain of youth," he says. "You can make the old young again."

I walk over and yank the remote from his hand. Hit the pause button and he stands. On the screen, Dawn is leaned back, her hands on the handlebars of the Big Wheel. Hair blown flat behind her.

He holds his hand out, his face vibrating. Eyes pink and slicked over.

"See what I'm saying," I say, and point. He looks at the screen. It twitches, trying to move forward. White lines jerk across the middle of his daughter. "The video wants to keep going," I tell him. "It has to. That's what it does." I take his hand and lay the remote in his palm. He looks at me, a tear beaded at the bottom of one eye, before it zips down. "Nature," I say, "takes its course."

He closes his fingers over the remote, sits down, and takes a drink. Hits play and his daughter leans forward, her hair dropping back flat.

In the video, next door is my mini backyard. My son's bicycle propped against the chain-link fence. The doghouse where no dog's lived since my wife left. Her withered Forget-me-nots are lifted and flipped by a breeze. For more years than I've got fingers, she groomed that flower garden. She sunbathed on the patio and we hosted barbecues for friends. The camera shaking, kids yelling, I try to rewind our life in my head—we're ignoring each other, just walking around backwards like erratic moving zombies.

Rewind.

We're screaming and fighting, her walking away toward me in the hall. Her upheld hands lowering.

Rewind.

We're making up before having small disagreements. Everything ending before it begins.

Jeff and Pam, my wife and I, we're taking food *out* of our mouths. Around the grill, the smoke vents down. The food un-cooks. Dawn and Kaden skip around in reverse.

Then, we're watching our son ride his new bike backwards. The dog running beside him, wagging tail first.

Then, we're staring at our backyard for the first time, before we back inside in quick jerks, wide smiles stretching narrow.

I blink and take another drink. On the video, the sky above the party's the color of soaked newspaper. Clouds clawing over each other. Wind blowing.

The camera looks down at Dawn, who's pulled in front of Jeff's feet. She smiles up, a front tooth missing. Her head cocked to the side.

The camera zooms in and Jeff's voice says: *Can I ride?*

Her head still cocked, Dawn closes her eyes, rolls her bottom lip over her top, and says: *You wish, blowfish.*

She peddles back from the camera, waving, then starts riding in circles. Jeff rewinds the tape and in quick time, she circles counterclockwise and stops, facing the camera. Rides toward the lens, smiling and waving, and stops at Jeff's feet. Her head cocks. Mouth moving, bottom lip rolled over top unrolling.

Her closed eyes open.

Jeff hits play and his voice says: *Can I ride?*

A tear rips over his smiling cheekbone and he says with his daughter, "You wish, blowfish."

The screen says: 02:08:49.

I sit beside him. Swallowing in quick bursts, my eyes sting. My face hurts. Tightens like a clinched fist. "Turn it off," I tell him. "Please?"

"With video," he says, his voice skipping, "you got the power to bring people back to life." He says, "Just by pressing a button—they're dead, then they're alive." He slides a hand through his hair, rubs it hard back and forth, and slips it out. He says, "Like an electronic God."

He starts to speak, stops, then tells me with the right timing, you can stop the *Challenger* from exploding. He says, "That teacher'll never make it to space, but she won't *not* make it, either."

The screen says: 02:09:21.

His voice shaking, he says, "You can stop bombs from hitting."

Remove cancer.

Reverse AIDS.

Barely audible, he says, "You can single fingerly control fate."

On the video, Dawn is still riding in circles. Her voice getting louder with each loop. The screen says: 2:10:10.

:13.

:15.

The wind picks up and Dawn throws her head back, laughing. Kaden chasing her around, hands Frankensteined out.

:17.

:19.

"Pause Buddy Holly's plane lifting away," he says, just breath and shaking voice, "and the music don't die."

:21.

:23.

And I put my arm around his neck, pull him toward me. He drops his head to my chest and his shoulders start to tremor. I slip the remote from his hand. I look at our yard, shaking in the background. Everything dark and dead or dying. I know video doesn't show the future. It can't make divorced couples married. Make sick people well. Make dead people alive.

You wish, blowfish.

I squint and the TV goes blurry.

On the video, a single raindrop pops the camera lens and slides down. Dawn finishes her loops and takes off down the driveway, toward the street. Peddling hard, the grind of plastic wheels over pavement.

And I hit the pause button, catching a voice in mid-scream. Camera in mid-shake. Freezing Pam in the middle of standing. Stopping Dawn from peddling into the street and away forever.

The screen twitches, trying to move forward. To do what's next.

"It don't die," he says, into my chest.

"It don't die," I say, wishing it were true.

# TONY HOZENY

## *SAFE FOR NOW*

Every Monday, Diane took care of their seventeen-month-old granddaughter Katie. At lunch time, Ken liked to come home from his CPA practice and play with Katie. Just now, she was banging her spoon on the highchair tray, hollering "eat, eat."

"It's coming, honey," Diane said, smiling as she gave her a bowl of macaroni and a tippy cup full of milk.

Ken leaned forward so Katie could pull his cap off his bald head, one of their favorite games. She giggled. Ken picked up her spoon and pretended to eat.

"I eat," she said, grabbing the spoon. Ken laughed. They loved to watch Katie concentrating hard and slowly bringing the spoon to her mouth. Each time she succeeded, Ken clapped or said, "Good girl!" Katie beamed.

When she was done, Ken lifted her out of the high chair. She slowly peeled off stickers and placed them on a sheet of drawing paper. Diane brought Ken a cup of coffee, a ham sandwich and a bowl of last night's potato salad. She sat down and rubbed her right knee.

"So, what did you do this morning?"

"We read books, and she played with her bear. She tried to get him to drink out of her cup."

Ken chuckled, reached down and patted Katie's back.

"Then we played hide and seek. She goes running around on her little legs and then she finds you and laughs and laughs. Those big Legos are great. See the tower we built?"

"Cute." He chewed his sandwich.

"Did you read about that school shooting in Arkansas? Four kids dead. Every time you turn around, there's another one. Nobody's doing a damned thing about it, either."

Ken scowled. "Why do you read stuff like that, Diane? How's your knee?"

"Please don't change the subject."

"They got the guy who did it, right?"

"The world used to be so much safer. What if I took Katie to the grocery store, and some maniac starts shooting up the place. How could I protect her?"

"Here we have a beautiful granddaughter, and all you can think about is negative stuff."

"Bock," said Katie, picking up a block.

"Green," Ken said. "Say 'green.'"

Katie dropped the block and crawled over to her yellow garbage truck. She ran it back and forth over the gray-and-blue throw rug.

"This is a safe area. Stop worrying. All this stuff goes in streaks. Remember five years ago, it was all gang violence? Now you never hear about it."

"It's still going on. Last week, I—"

"Diane." Ken shook his head. "Just drop it. I have to get back to my mountain of taxes. Probably be a little late tonight." He bent down and kissed Katie on the forehead and rubbed her black curly hair. "Say 'bye, bye, grandpa.'"

"Bye bye," Katie said.

He left without kissing Diane goodbye.

Katie was good about lying still, so it was an easy diaper change. Diane wished Ken would listen instead of mouthing platitudes. But he ignored anything that didn't directly affect him. Since she'd retired from the clinic two months ago, they were bickering more and more. She wondered if Katie could feel the tension between them.

"How about a book, Katie?"

Katie grabbed a book, then another, and threw it to the floor. "No, no," Diane said. Katie knocked down the Lego tower. Diane looked out the window. A weak sun shone through the thin clouds. The backyard was snow-streaked, too muddy for play, but they could take a short walk up the sidewalk.

"Come on, Katie, let's go outside."

Big smile. Katie toddled over the the door and put on her pink shoes. For the first time, she was able to pull over and secure the Velcro straps. Diane hugged her and kissed her and told her how proud she was. She helped Katie into her coat and wool hat and grabbed a jacket for herself.

"Take Grandma's hand now, Katie."

Katie grabbed Diane's index finger and held on. Diane's knee clicked and ached with every step, but she liked the chance for a little adventure with Katie. Katie toddled along, brown eyes wide, taking in everything. Their street, which climbed a steep hill, seemed a lot busier than usual, one car after another. Katie pointed at a bus. Diane said, "Bus."

Diane heard a car coming too fast before she could see it. It careened over the crest of the hill and headed down, a blur. Katie broke free, hollering "no hand," and half-toddled, half-ran up the block. Diane followed, reaching, hollering, "No, no, Katie, come back to grandma!" Tires howling, motor roaring, cloud of bitter blue smoke, the car jumped the curb with a terrifying thump, aiming straight at them. Diane grabbed for Katie, missed, pushed off on her right foot and scooped her up, and together they toppled onto the grass. The car spun out a shower of mud and snow and lurched back onto the road away from them.

Diane held Katie tight, kissing her and kissing her, thanking God. Pain sliced though her knee and ripped up and down her leg. But all that mattered was Katie safe in her arms. After a minute, Katie began squirming and wiggling.

"No, no, you stay with grandma."

Katie lay back in Diane's arms. Then she giggled.

"I fall down," she said. "Gomma fall down." She giggled again. "Fun!"

"That's right, darling." She kissed Katie's head. "We fall down, all right."

"Fun!" Their eyes met. Katie giggled. Diane laughed and laughed and laughed.

## CHRIS ELLERY

*SILENT*

Whoever heard of night
using big words
to get what it wanted?
Star light comes to you
caroling, but there are
no words or music.

When you climb to the top,
you don't expect
the mountain to lecture.
Wind in an icy crevice
explains nothing that you think
needs explaining.

The tongues of flame that took
my father and mother
had nothing to say.
Because I was silent
and listened, I heard
the lesson and learned it.

## A SMALL BLUE FLAME

In the middle of the thunderstorm my plumber calls
me from across the street to tell me
Half your roof is gone. Yeah I said I heard it go
and wondered to myself What do you do
in the middle of a storm when your plumber calls
to tell you half your roof is gone?

Pinned fast to a spinning panic, I pause. I listen.
Yes, I, who so rarely listen, listened.
The storm says Isn't it obvious? You fall
in love with something. Quick. Maybe
with the small force of the blue flame
that lights the hot water heater whenever
the hot water heater needs lighting.
Or with the mouse you can barely hear
still scratching in the wall over the noise
of your house dying violently.

Really almost anything will do.

                              For a year once
I admired a girl on the same bus.
I was a rodent scratching on the wall
of adolescence, too much a mouse to love her.
My mind kept telling me No, my little human ego,
weak as a wisp of straw in the wind,
forbidding me with thunderous arguments
the F5 blow of her rebuff.
She was too flawless, too rare, too beautiful
up there, two grades above me
in the striations of the supercell.
So I stopped myself from falling.

Hard as a chunk of ice hitting the earth,
I stopped myself.

But why should I stop now? I ask,
now with the storm raging,
now that a hostile wind
is fighting with lumber and nails to carry me
in pieces to a different state?

I guess you wonder if it's easy
to fall in love with something, anything,
inside a thunderstorm.
A girl, a mouse, a flame. Maybe even
(strangest thing) perhaps your wife,
a stranger these many years,
now calmly comforting your fetal children
while junk from thirty counties
beats against the walls at a hundred miles an hour.

Well, I promise I will tell you, if I make it through
in more or less one piece.
I'll tell you if a storm gives advice worth listening to.
I'll tell if it was easy.
I'll tell you how I cowered on the floor in the hall
of my shuddering house
and did or did not do, for once,
what I could never do.

## MARY JUMBELIC

### *THAT KID*

I channeled what my mentor had taught me as I sat rigid on the witness stand. In my forensic pathology training, when I had asked my chief how he handled the tough cross-examinations, he said, "You've got to remember, you're the doctor." As I stared at the attorney who was expecting my answer, being the coroner's physician didn't feel very helpful.

"Can you answer the question or not?" she said. She stood behind the defense table and gripped the edge.

The courtroom was quiet, just a few observers, the attorneys, the defendants, the judge, and me. There was no jury; this was a bench trial.

"I don't know," I said.

"You don't know if you can answer the question or is that your answer?" She sparred.

Her line of questioning had taken an abrupt departure from the case. I was an expert witness in a trial of caretakers charged with medical negligence. I had autopsied an elderly woman and determined the cause of death to be sepsis related to untreated bed sores on her back: open and gaping, allowing bacteria to spread to her blood, and her organs to shut down.

"Can you repeat the question?" I said. This was my signal that trouble lay ahead. If I said it in response to the lawyer who requested my opinion in court, it meant "Are you sure you want the answer to that question?" If I said it to the opposing counsel, it was a trigger for the other attorney to object. No one picked up on this.

"Okay, Doctor." She smiled. "Isn't it possible for someone to have a widespread infection and a caretaker not to recognize the severity?" She was the lawyer for the middle-aged couple who claimed they never saw a bed sore on the woman. At autopsy the wound cavity was deep, down to bone over the sacrum, and putrefying. The defense theory seemed to be that anyone can miss a life-threatening infection, even licensed caregivers.

Experience taught me not to engage attorneys in hypothetical battles. The speculative information provided never had the detail obtained in real forensic investigations. When I expressed a professional opinion in a death, I relied on data, not concocted notions to suit the circumstance. Lawyers dealt in minute possibilities; medical examiners dealt in credible probabilities.

"I don't know," I said. "In what circumstance? Where was the inciting injury? Was it visible? What type of infection? Who was the caregiver? Who was the patient? Could they express discomfort?" My questions streamed like a magician pulling endless handkerchiefs from the mouth. Still, no one objected. "I need comprehensive information to form an opinion."

I looked over at the prosecution, hoping they recognized this vague and broad line of questioning should be invalid.

Opposing counsel's smile didn't falter. She leaned ever more forward toward the witness stand; her eyes bore into me.

"Okay, let's get specific," she said. "You took your son to the hospital yesterday because he had an unrecognized infection, isn't that true?" She didn't wait for my answer. "You missed his infection, didn't you, Doctor?"

Tears filled my eyes and spilled down my cheeks. Her outline blurred. No one had ever talked about my family in a court of law. It felt like I had stopped breathing. I turned to the judge.

"I need to use the bathroom," I said. I had never cried on the witness stand or had any excuse to interrupt my testimony; in the years that followed, I never did again.

"Objection," said the prosecutor. It sounded like he was objecting to my need for the bathroom.

I didn't wait for the judge's reply but hurried from the courtroom. The door banged behind me. I sat on the toilet in the ladies' room in my suede gray suit. My head dropped to my knees.

"Dr. J?" The female prosecutor stood outside the stall.

"How did she know?" I said.

"When we delayed the trial yesterday, I told her why," she said. "I never thought she would bring it up in court."

I had spent the day before with my son, David, at the hospital. He had an overwhelming infection in his hand and needed emergency surgery and intravenous antibiotics. I stayed overnight with him, hardly sleeping, and showed up in court earlier this day.

"I am not going back in there," I said, sounding like a spoiled child refusing to go to school. "She had no right, no right at all." My sobs continued.

"She was out of line. I'll have a sidebar and explain to the judge. We have a fifteen minute break. Come into my office when you're ready."

I felt violated: my personal life used against me in the hallowed halls of justice. What did my son have to do with this? Beneath it all, I felt guilt too.

The infection had begun with a childhood accident, the little finger of David's three-year-old left hand nearly amputated by a pair of Joyce Chen scissors, strong enough to cut chicken bone but lightweight and easy to handle, wielded by his five-year-old brother, Joshua.

My husband, Marc, and the boys were out flying kites on a sunny autumn day while I was at work. Marc had brought the scissors in case he had to untangle the monofilament string. While he was exclaiming how beautiful the crimson diamond-shape looked in the sky, Joshua cut the grass with the scissors. David reached down to take a turn.

David screamed and ran toward his father; the left hand covered in red. Marc told me later that he was disoriented and thought the kite had come down when he saw all that red. Joshua was crying, too, with his breathing coming quickly, the beginning of an asthma attack. As Marc scooped David into his arms, he recognized the trauma and pulled off his sweatshirt to make a tourniquet. Grabbing Joshua around the waist, he managed to carry both boys to the car, then rushed to the hospital. He didn't call me until everybody had settled in the ER.

That had been nearly a week ago. A hand surgeon reattached the finger that had been dangling by a tendril of skin. The end of David's hand was covered by sturdy plaster of Paris; the protective wrapping obscured the fingers. The bandaging safeguarded the delicate microsurgery, making the digit invisible.

David had the persona of Curious George: "kinetic" was how the Montessori teachers described him. One day at school, he dropped an apple in a toilet and retrieved it with his injured hand. He kept this incident a secret, only relating it much, much later to his dad and me.

We readied for trick or treating. David played the role of a pirate, a recycled costume of Joshua's. In a photo of that day, he appears jaunty even with the cast. He wears a black eyepatch, and red and white striped shirt, fringed at the waist and the cuffs. If I look carefully, he seems flushed and his face a little puffy, but grinning broadly. David claimed Halloween his favorite Jewish holiday.

The next morning Namma, as the boys affectionately called my mother, and I rushed around getting them dressed and preparing breakfast. David kept asking for his treats from the night before. I usually drove the kids to preschool. As I pulled the pajama shirt over David's head, his skin felt hot. Quickly I palpated the lymph nodes in his left armpit, which were swollen to the size of grapes. Medical alarms rang in my head. I knew that his finger had a serious infection and it had spread to his body. The cast precluded me checking his digit.

"Mom," I said from the bedroom.

Namma had been cleaning up but came up the stairs at my call.

"I have to take David to the emergency room. We need the doctor to look at his finger." I didn't want to alarm her but needed her to understand the urgency.

"Okay, Mary, I'll take Joshie to school."

"Thanks."

"Where are we going?" said David, not sounding his exuberant self.

"The hospital." I said. "We'll get the cast off and check your hand. You have a little fever." I always felt compelled to tell the truth to my boys.

"Yea," he said, eternally the optimist and thinking this meant freedom for his hand.

That had been twenty-four hours earlier. Since then, his little finger, looking like a rotting Bob Evans pork link, had been surgically debrided, cleaned up, and rewrapped in the operating room. The doctor couldn't tell me if the original microsurgery was harmed or not. David received heavy doses of multiple antibiotics. He lay in a hospital bed with Namma, Marc and I taking turns by his side. I had spent the night and headed straight to court.

After leaving the bathroom, I followed the prosecuting attorney back to her office. She let me sit there while she had a discussion with the other lawyer and the judge. I don't remember how I returned to the courtroom or even the rest of my testimony. There were no more questions about my son or allusions to my ignorance as a caretaker. I was probably on the stand only another few minutes. The delay in seeking care for David's hand weighed heavily upon me.

Marc, Namma, and I rotated shifts at the hospital. Within a week, my son returned home. He had a Broviac catheter in his chest so he could receive double antibiotics three times a day through its intravenous port directly into his heart. I performed all the treatments at home, using sterile technique, masks, and gloves. David had to mask up, too, since the line lay just inches from his face.

This aggressive regimen treated the bacteria that had gone deep into his bone. The doctors wanted to avoid amputation. The therapy also involved weekly blood draws to check David's white blood cell count and any other sign of continuing infection. This lasted for three months.

I relished the time snuggled next to David, surrounded by bags of fluids and drugs, listening to audiocassette recordings of children's books, the kind that beep to signal when to turn the page. Our favorite was *Plants of Peril* featuring Batman and Poison Ivy. The beautiful villainess escaped Gotham Penitentiary on the first page but ended up captured by Batman and returned to her cell in the end. Maybe it was an allegory for wanting freedom yet needing structure. I held him close.

On the final day of blood testing, David refused to get out of the car. No amount of pleading, bargaining, or explaining had any effect. Finally, I just had to carry him into the clinic. He squirmed and cried.

A pediatric nurse, familiar with toddlers, deftly took him from my arms. I followed them into the treatment room. Two staff members placed him onto the examination table and harnessed him with thick leather straps, like something out of *One Flew Over the Cuckoo's Nest*. The room decorations belied this with primary-color clowns cavorting on the walls. Afterwards we went home in a somber mood.

A few days later, David had his final medical visit with the infectious disease specialist: the three months of intravenous antibiotic therapy over. Lab results had normalized. The doctor removed the chest catheter. As the physician filled out paperwork, I tilted David's face up to mine to give him a kiss. I froze.

"What is in your nose?" I said.

David put his right index finger to his left nostril.

I bent his head further back and looked. A yellow fuse bead winked at me.

"David."

He managed to try to look chagrined. I swallowed.

"Doctor," I said, my voice quavering. "We have a new problem." I explained that my son had stuck a bead up his nose, the polyethylene kind used to make a design on a pegboard to be heated and made into permanent art. Joshua and David had brought their creations home from school recently:

a duck and a smiley face. The beads were non-toxic, safe for children, made of food grade material but not meant for noses.

"We'll have to call ENT and take him over there. Maybe they can remove it as an outpatient procedure. Otherwise, he'll have to go to the ER," the doctor said. He gathered David's file.

"Wait," I said. "Do you have a hemostat? Locking forceps? Can't you just take it out? I can see it clearly."

"Oh, no, no, no." He seemed to back away. "I'm a specialist."

We looked at each other.

"Do you have a hemostat? Just get me a hemostat."

Seeing the yellow bead emboldened me despite his reluctance. David sat unusually still on the exam table.

The doctor reached into a nearby drawer and retrieved a packaged sterile instrument.

"Gloves," I spoke as if the doctor were my assistant. "Shine your penlight here."

I put on the surgical gloves and opened the package of the hemostat. In less than a second, I had the complete bead out with no bleeding.

"Thanks, Mommy," David said. "It hurt."

# IV
# QUOTIDIAN

# *WONDER AT THE SMALL CONNECTIONS*

# RICHARD LEBLOND

## *THE NATURAL MOMENT*

This has been an unusually busy winter for me. What used to be a given—a daily walk in the outer Cape Cod woods—has become a luxury. There is meager compensation from being too busy to fret about it.

But prolonged absences can make us more receptive to what is known as the natural moment. This is a sudden, unexpected event, such as an encounter with an animal or a sound out of the blue. It is a moment that has the form if not the content of revelation. The mind is instantly ushered from its internal rumination to a state of external awareness. It is a wake-up call.

One recent night I took our dog outside for his last chance before bed. It was a calm night, warm for early spring, and not a cloud in the sky. While the dog frantically searched for that perfect place, I sat down on the bench we had rescued from a junk heap at a Hyannis pond. It was while sitting on the bench that I was hit broadside by the natural moment.

As so often happens, the moment was generated by a sound. It was neither a loud nor a sudden sound, and had been there all along, unnoticed. It crept up behind and leaped into my awareness, and for a few moments I experienced a state of higher consciousness, a mind disconnected from its preoccupations and reconnected with the world around it. It was one of those moments during which a sense of time and place is simultaneously pinpointed and obliterated.

The source of the sound was the ocean; specifically, the sound of heavy surf on the outer beach two miles away. The previous day we had been visited by a Nor'easter, and though the wind was gone, the sea continued to thrash the shore, releasing stored energy. The sound of the surf, though distant and of few decibels, was nonetheless huge and primal. It was a sound I had heard many times before, but this time there was something in it that seemed out of ancient memory, a sound originally heard from the other side of the surf, from within the sea.

The natural moment was further elaborated by the arrival of a second sound, that of a foghorn. There was no need for a foghorn on such a clear and windless night, and I fancied that this sound, like the waves, was a product of yesterday's storm, disconnected and tossed about, a false hope for a lost mariner.

Not all sudden or unexpected sounds result in the natural moment. Some produce the unnatural moment, and these most often are of human origin, usually mechanical. Nowhere is one entirely free of them. Even in remote wilderness airplanes can be heard or their vapor trails seen.

But origin is relative, and whether a stimulus is mind-expanding or annoying isn't always determined by whether it was produced by nature or by man. The nearest I have come to prolonged experiences of only natural sounds has been during lengthy stays in a dune shack. Yet one of my favorite sounds in that solitude happens at night, under the quilt, listening to the distant putter of fishing boats. They sound like giant faraway butterflies with piston-driven wings.

A wondrous mockingbird provided my favorite dune moment. The bird was on the other side of a cranberry bog, in a beach plum thicket. I was only partly listening to it when it mimicked the call of a Fowler's toad. That caught my full attention, so I sat down on the lower slope of the dune on my side of the bog. This bird did each call twice, then went on to the next. He focused on the dune aviary, but allowed the occasional shorebird, and mimicked another dune toad, the American. But his *tour de force* was not the mimicry of a natural sound at all. He perfectly captured the muted sound of a semi-truck passing on Route 6 a mile away, immediately followed by the passing of a second truck. Then he continued with his accounting of the dune aviary. After that, a mile-away truck became one of my favorite sounds in the dunes. It had become the call of a mockingbird.

But back to the foghorn we left adrift a few moments ago. It and two cohorts were responsible for another of my favorite natural moments on Cape Cod. It was an August day in 1974, after I had just returned from a two-year absence. I was standing on the low bluff that sits between Village Pond and Cape Cod Bay in North Truro, refreshing my memory. I was wondering why the foghorns at Race Point, Wood End, and Long Point were sounding on such a clear day when all of a sudden the three of them bellowed at once.

For those of you familiar with such things, it was in more ways than one a major chord. I later asked our resident composer about this phenomenon.

He too had become familiar with the foghorn tones, though had never heard them in unison. He described the three tones as a second inversion A-flat major triad.

The most distant horn was eight miles away, meaning that a very large area was momentarily bathed in a rich, harmonious music. It had all the earmarks of the best natural moments: unexpected, coincidental, and mind-expanding.

The Coast Guard employs a foghorn tuner. It is his job to make sure each horn has a distinctive tone for identification. I just had to call him, and he said the major triad (second inversion) was unintended. He has since rescored the music to a dissonant chord, also without intent. That's as it should be. Part of me would have loved to hear that huge music again and again. But the memory of the moment would have been lost in the repetition.

## BONNI CHALKIN

### *A BREATH IN TIME*

None of this looks familiar. It's like I'm being hijacked into a world I don't know. I was looking at the same semi-paved road that I had traveled every day for the past fifteen years with large spruce forests on either side, which allowed only a glimmer of the sun to find its way through. Suddenly it all seemed foreign. Today, I recognized none of it. What was all so familiar to me became a landscape of the unknown. It was as if I looked at the palm of my hand and my fortune had changed. The scent of those tremendous trees, their secret whispers, embraced me in a way that I had never experienced before. It awakened me, energized me. It seemed the wind aroused everything in its path, including me.

Those are the moments. The ones that can't be described. The ones that show you there really is something so much bigger than you. You feel truly in the moment and time stands still. It took my breath away as tears flowed down my cheeks from the immersion of true joy that filled every cell of my body. I didn't move.

I wanted it to last forever.

# LENORE BALLIRO

## *PAUSING*

1.
Because I have no deadline, because my watch is inside out, because I do not have to catch a train or a bus, because no one is waiting anywhere to embrace me, because embracing—Because there is no one waiting for me to drive somewhere, because there is nowhere to go, because I already took out the recycling and paid the bills, because the woods still have trails, I can let the dog off leash to sniff at coded aromas, I can stretch out on a slab of granite in the grout pile, warmed by a skeptical sun, and look up at the canopy of trees above me, where hesitant birds start their spring calls—Because it is the cusp, the sky is unsure, because the dog's eyes have moved from fear to pleading to acceptance, because it is the cusp, and hesitant birds start their spring calls, because I think that they will sing to me.

2.
If you sit quietly and let yourself. Sometimes a sentence fragment is just the thing. Listen to the click, swish of individual leaves on a palm frond. Especially if dusk is settling and you are far from home. Especially if home has no context for you now. Roosters crow and goats butt their kids in the adjacent field. But back to the palm fronds. Look up. In a gentle breeze, each slender leaf in the palm frond moves like piano keys played by a man with the gentlest of fingertips, who understands. We are trying too hard to grasp the global. When all along, the click, swish and symmetry of movement is revealed every evening, under a silver sky, under a gentle mist that can rinse you. If you sit quietly and let yourself.

3.
Rain comes down hard on the river. Three kayakers shift their tempo. Paddles slap fast. Masks in the backpacks. The young ones laugh, still in love, race

ahead. The elder, stiff from quarantined muscles, lags behind. Sees the spotted turtles bereft of sun plop back under the water's surface. Sees a ball of fur and bone caught in a web of branches, vague remains that ripple with the current. Closes her eyes, invites lightening to choose her. Rests paddles against her lap. Tilts her head back, gray hair heavy with rain, dripping down her back. Opens her mouth for a last sip from the darkening heavens.

4.
Sun skateboards across the cove, sparkling the edges of wavelets like methamphetamine crystals. I don't want to break bad, but still. The sky turns the color of acute embarrassment, everything slows as the sun makes its downward move. Our limbs take on weight. Later, a woman returns to walk an old dog off leash. I watch from afar as she picks the newly exposed moon off the horizon and hides it in her pocket. She knows things will go dark fast, and she'll need just enough light to guide the stray dog back to safety.

5
At Lydgate Beach Park, toward sunset, local families gather for supper. They set up grills, blankets, chairs, baskets of food. A shallow space encircled by volcanic rock protects *keki* from harsh waves. Time shifts, slows down. The sun sheds benevolence. I head for the water to swim and greet the surgeonfish beneath the surface: large, blue, small yellow fins. They surprise me by swimming underneath my body. I am buoyed by joy. My heart swells and shrinks at the same time. I flashback to summers in Maine, when my girl was so young, and we clutched at a happiness we thought would last.

6
Walking alongside Kuamo'o Road, mid-day. Creatures skitter into the switchgrass as they sense my footsteps. Soft rustles. A truck rises up from the weeds. Roosters claim dominion. Slight detour brings me to the Hindu Temple, closed now, but a quiet, cool resting spot outside invites me to breathe. I am glad there is no internet access. I am glad I am sweating. I am glad thinking of the anoles, lizards, geckos that skitter into the switchgrass. They also call it panic grass. I wad up my panic and toss it into the bed of the weed truck on my way back to the Homesteads, before I dive into the clear salt water at Lydgate, deep, my body joining the big blue fish, ground feeders, waiting for me.

## RUSS ALLISON LOAR

### *ZERO*

Zero,
Ever been there?
I hear the weather's nice
This time of year.

I was there last fall,
Just in time to see no leaves changing no colors on no trees.
So beautiful,
Like nothing I'd ever seen before.

The trip was a little rough,
And long.
Just when it seemed like Zero was in sight,
Along came something else
And my curiosity would get the better of me,
Stopping to explore one thing after another.

But finally,
After a very long day full of starts and stops,
After I was completely worn out,
After I had just about enough of everything,
There it was:
Zero.

So beautiful,
Like nothing I'd ever seen before.

## A PURPLE SHOELACE

As I walk toward the growing darkness
Along the sunset trail,
The last of the after-hour walkers pass me by,
Returning to their parked cars
And nightly routines.

Many are deep in determined conversation
With walking partners or cellphone voices.
Others are earbud oblivious,
Even to their over-eager dogs,
Straining at the leash.

I am alone in silence,
Bearing witness to the last auburn rays of light
Retreating from nearby hillsides,
Earlier each day now.
I hear rustling leaves whisper the coming of autumn.

And there,
One lost purple shoelace,
Tied to a chain-link fence.

## *ALL I KNOW ABOUT LOVE I LEAVE*

All I know about love I leave
Outside the door to your room.
Inside, raw passion will do,
The electric feel of skin touching skin,
Wanting yet waiting,
Teasing,
Playing.

Like the blind our fingers have sight
As we move in love's rhythms,
Tossed by the sea of night.

And all that mattered a few hours before
And all that waits outside your door
Matters no more.

## QUIET MOMENTS

These quiet moments
When alone I become my truer self,
My unguarded self,
Finger in nose,
Unrestrained flatulence,
Indelicate scratching,
Cursing trivial inconveniences
With profane language I would never use
In the presence of family or friends.

These quiet moments,
Beset by erratic, uncaged thoughts,
Past-life recriminations,
Indulgent, forbidden impulses.

This hidden core,
This embryo untouched by civility,
Unbound,
Disdainful of all my life's accumulated lessons,
Disconnected from the cloak of identity I have made.
This dark beast will not die.

## MARY KAY RUMMEL

## WINTER SOLSTICE IN BIG SUR

*Between every tree and its story*
*is an opening to night*

I want to bend down
to taste the sacred minerals.

I send up prayers
and they float away.

*Between every dance*
*of air is a departure*

Raising my arms
I face the moon and bow
breathing with trees
in the circle of redwoods.

Their silence—a murmuration,
a wave of evergreen and pine
surrounds my fear
fills my emptiness.

*Between every circle and its rim*
*is a call lapping at the roots*

I hear this call
the way I sense the cold path
when clouds obscure the moon
then clear above the circled crowns
of thousand year old redwoods.

Through the high branches
a passage for solstice light,
ring of planets,
corona of black, of gold and rose
makes the old moon young.

*Between mountains and rivers of wind*
*a tree shivers at the edge*

Night shadows
I cannot know
but there is time, still, to search
for translucence,
the pearl-sheen of life.

*Between insomnia and sleep*
*trees singing in cold air*

songs only the old and very young can hear.

# TERRY DALRYMPLE

## *OUR VAST AND PRESENT MOMENT*

Mary Louise Shaw, home from her second job, saw the scene she had come to expect. Her husband sat in his easy chair, beer in hand, fat cigar protruding from his mouth. The apartment reeked from the smoke. Five crushed beer cans had been tossed onto the coffee table, along with Chinese take-out cartons, one of which had tipped over and oozed brown liquid onto the table. When she passed his chair, he slanted his eyes toward her. She responded with a brief nod and kept walking. She didn't bother stepping into the kitchen, knowing all too well that he wouldn't think of getting take-out for her. But it didn't matter. She knew the routine and had eaten a sandwich at the bistro where she waited tables after a day of clerking at the department store.

In her room—her husband had months before begun sleeping in his easy chair in the living room—she unzipped her dress, let it fall, and stepped out of the puddle of material. She flopped into her chair by the window. She was bone tired. From working two jobs for a total of sixteen hours, yes, but also from her dreary life. Just once, she thought, I'd like to feel happy again, alive again, and I'd like to see beauty again.

When they first married, she felt happy and alive always. He had ambitions and the energy, he claimed, to fulfill them. She wanted a house by the lake and eagerly anticipated the day they could afford one. But even now they still lived in a one-bedroom apartment a mile or more from the lake. His first business venture had failed utterly, and slowly that failure sucked up his ambition and energy. He worked part-time at the box factory, where he stood at a conveyor belt and watched for damaged or misshapen products, which he would remove and toss into a large bin behind him. He swore he was trying but simply couldn't get on full time or find another, better job. He had simply given up.

She stood and stepped to the window. At least their third-floor apartment provided a distant view of the calm lake water. She stared at it and the lights reflected on its surface. She longed to live right on its shore. She heard dogs, or maybe coyotes, yapping and howling somewhere near the lake. Damned animals, she thought, disturbing the quiet evening in the pursuit of prey or in fear of danger. She sighed and fell back into the chair. Then, she changed her mind, stood, slipped her panties off, unhooked her bra, and dropped it on top of the panties. Nudity was the closest she could come to feeling free and unencumbered. She sat and sucked in a deep breath.

※ ※ ※

On the other side of town in a large, two-story house overlooking the lake, Robert "Shake" Perkins sipped slowly on his scotch, neat, the single drink he allowed himself each evening. It would help him sleep later. The evening news, volume turned low, lit his television screen, but he paid little attention, instead appreciating the large, framed photo of his wife. He had the photo enlarged and framed after her funeral. That had been almost a year before, and he still missed her desperately. He liked gazing at the photo and remembering their years together.

He knew that sadness was nothing new and certainly nothing unique. He had practiced family law for the past forty-two years and was no stranger to the many forms of jealousy, anger, sadness, disappointment, and loneliness of which the human heart is capable. And he was no exception, especially after his wife died. He had come to dislike his job but kept working because it was all he had to distract himself from himself, to fill his time. He longed for her laughter, her optimism, her ability to find beauty in virtually everything. He sipped his last bit of scotch, used the remote to darken the television. He arose and trudged upstairs to their bedroom. No, just his bedroom now. Unbuttoning his shirt, he looked out the window at the lake, a view she had always thrilled to. Moonlight and starlight shimmered on its surface, but he felt no thrill.

※ ※ ※

Downtown, a teenage boy, Billy Norwood, ran a maze of dark alleys and side streets trying to evade the police officers who had come to get him. His breath weakened the longer he ran, and eventually he slowed to a trot, then to a vigorous walk. Stupid, he thought. Why was I so stupid? He had tried to buy the bottle of bourbon, sure that he wouldn't be carded. But the clerk turned out to be diligent. When the man asked for his ID, the boy just looked down and said nothing.

"Okay, kid," the clerk said. "Move along."

But the kid—he—had been stupid. He had grabbed the bottle and sprinted for the door. He glanced back to see the clerk already on the phone.

Finally, he stopped and bent, hands on knees, to catch his breath. Even if the police didn't find him, the clerk had gotten a good look. The cops would come, and his parents would let him sit in jail for a couple days before bailing him out. Damn. Why didn't he just walk away? Why did he grab that bottle? He had no answer. At the mouth of an alley, he threw the bottle into a dumpster and headed home, dreading his arrival. When he stepped into the street, the light surprised him. It was an unlit street, but the moon and stars shone brighter than a streetlamp. He looked up and admired them.

On the far side of the lake, a cardinal, out unusually late, perched on a short rock wall along a walking path. Its head bobbed up toward the sky, then down toward the lake, then side to side.

Mary Louise Shaw, in the drowse of almost-sleep, pushed herself up out of her chair. But before stumbling to bed, she once again stepped to the window. A full white moon hung high above the lake, its reflection brilliant. Far beyond the moonlight, bright stars dotted the darkness. She heard the dogs or coyotes. They weren't hunting, she thought, or confronting danger. They were barking at the moon, celebrating this moment when it shone so brightly. The brightness of stars and moon mesmerized her, and she knew that beyond her sight more stars shone, other moons orbited other planets, all of them moving, circling, swirling, as they did day after day, night after night. They knew nothing of sadness or pain, they never paused, they simply swirled through a forever present moment. She felt awestruck by them, by this moment. And suddenly she wanted to share the moment with her husband.

Like her, he, too, was troubled, sad, lonely, defeated, and she desperately wanted to call him to the window, to say, "Look at this moment." This moment, all moments. Not the past, not the future, just this moment and every moment of their lives. It was vast and it was now, now and always. It was a vast and present moment. Everyone's vast and present moment, she thought. Our vast and present moment. She felt calm, peaceful, blessed by the whole unfathomable universe. She murmured a prayer that everyone everywhere would know that moment, would feel that peace.

At that same moment, Robert "Shake" Preston, in his pajamas, pulling back the bed covers, felt an urge to return to the window. He fixed his eyes on the lake and the beautiful way it reflected the night sky, and he felt that his wife was looking with him, smiling, thrilled by the view. Of course she was with him, he realized, always with him, reveling in the exact moment of her place and time. He knew he would sleep well.

Admiring the night sky, Billy Norwood didn't move. Soon, he would. He would go home, tell his parents what he did, spend a couple days locked up if he had to. But he would never miss another chance to enjoy moments like this. And he understood that moments like this were all moments if he just relaxed and stopped being stupid.

The cardinal opened its wings and flew farther up into the sky than it had ever been, then swooped low over the lake in a blur of red.

# IDENTITY

# JAMES SILAS ROGERS

## *LISTENING AT THE RAGGED EDGE OF SPRING*

When I was fourteen years old and almost through with eighth grade at St Augustine's grade school, I—like many boys in their early teens—conceived of myself as a deep thinker, and struck a pose as an intellectual. It still embarrasses me to realize how many books I carried around with no intention of reading, but with the wish that those who saw me would say, *he's deep*.

In reality, of course, I was a fourteen-year-old boy, retreating into this pose because I feared the more urgent business of adolescence: girls, social events, sports. I was a smart kid, no doubt, but not as smart as I thought I was, and if I were writing an intellectual autobiography I would have to say that the biggest influence on my "thinking" (if you want to call it that) was folk music. My classmates were enjoying rock 'n' roll, but I was a faithful listener to a nightly show called "The Folk Bag." I knew who Cisco and Woody had been, who Rambling Jack Elliott was, and I admired their rejection of bourgeois life, the hard-bitten authenticity of their lives among the working class.

From this romanticized vision, I deduced a corollary—that the real stuff of life was to be found in the run-down and the derelict. My attraction to the dilapidated was, I now realize, voyeuristic. My father was a bank officer. I went to a private school. We lived in a split-level suburban home. At fourteen, I had not so much as hitchhiked, let alone hopped a freight. But however inchoate the thinking, these ideas appealed to me. I would not have known what the Ashcan School was, but I had inherited its ethos.

My grade school in South St. Paul stood atop a hill, and at the bottom of that hill were plenty of run-down buildings to indulge my taste for neglected places. I used to head down the hill after school to Concord Street and walk on the railroad tracks, but never went any further. I have a vivid memory of one of these walks, which I can date with accuracy to the last week of March, 1967.

Concord Street and the tracks were lines of demarcation. Beyond the tracks, Swift's meat-packing plant was off-limits, protected by security guards. But I was near enough to that industrial background to imagine a picture of myself in such a setting that might appear on the cover of a folk album, covers showing Tom Rush stooping to light a cigarette above a railyard, Phil Ochs standing by the dock pilings, Bob Dylan in his denim work shirt. I must have been the only teenaged boy in America who was more intrigued by the fire escapes on the cover of *The Freewheelin' Bob Dylan* than by Susie Rotolo clutching his arm.

At the main intersection, Concord Street and Grand Avenue, the Quality Drug store anchored one of the corners. A cheap hotel—a flophouse called the Coates—operated on the second floor of the building, and I knew that at one time it had been a respectable place because my grandmother had known the manager at her church; he had the fortuitous name of Capps, making him Mr. Capps of the Coates. I certainly never stepped foot in it or in any of the other hotels along the street, some of which I later learned were known as haunts for prostitutes. But I visited Quality Drug often. A fine soda fountain stood at the back of the store, where I would stop for a cherry coke or lime phosphate. Innocence meeting experience: someone else's experience, though, that of the workingmen and women for whom this was daily life.

Up the hill from the drugstore, kitty-corner from the new municipal building, was a body shop, a gray building with almost no windows and the smell of spray paint.

I never entered the body shop, as I had no interest in cars. I walked behind it often, though, because part of my interest in dereliction was a belief that the backside of a building was more honest than the front (which, to be fair, might be true). Halfway up the hill, the back of the Schult Building had a wooden loading dock that thrust out into a parking lot. Another early adolescent fantasy: I envisioned it as a good performance space if one set up chairs in the parking lot—though of course, at fourteen, I had no idea of what would be performed or who might attend.

Behind the body shop was an undeveloped hillside covered with scrub trees, at the top of which was a limestone retaining wall that tilted backward and also fit the contour of the slope, probably four feet high at the south end and fifteen feet at the north end. Someone, who knows how long before, had put careful effort into building the wall. Sponge-like patches of moss grew along the small ledges in the wall.

I had been poking around down by the railroad tracks, and was cutting through the trees on a muddy trail below the retaining wall, headed for the library where I would call my mom to come pick me up. On the day I am remembering—and this is how I know it was the end of March—all the snow had melted. The Chinese elms and box elders were bare—unlovely trees, just woody weeds really, and absent their leaves especially unattractive. But on this day at the ragged edge of spring, they suited the rawness of the season.

In her fragmentary autobiography, *Moments of Being*, Virginia Woolf recalls scattered instances in her early life when she apprehended the world with a sort of heightened consciousness: a flower that seemed alive, a childhood moment when she stood on a chair and peered into a looking-glass. These are rare islands in experience in which we drop out of one timescale and into another, touching the underlying connectedness of everything. As Woolf says, perhaps we treasure these "Moments of Being" because they come to us so deeply embedded in the rest of our lives comprising "Moments of Non-Being."

And maybe such moments are better understood as grace.

I stood there in the cooling afternoon—it was that point in a spring late afternoon when the chilliness of the coming night asserts itself, and the sun drops in minutes—when I heard a truck pulling out of the stockyards. I decided to listen until I could no longer hear the muffler of the unseen truck.

It slowed down as it crossed the Chicago Great Western railroad tracks that paralleled the stockyards, accelerated briefly as it passed Aller's Café and the Exchange Building, then creaked through the left turn onto Concord Street. Maybe there was an unusual lack of ambient noise, or maybe the mufflers were louder than usual, but I had no trouble following the sound as the truck headed south on Concord. It would have been a mile away when I could tell it was slowing to go up the cloverleaf ramp onto Highway 110, past the Golden Steer Motel. And then it began gaining speed again, headed east, up the slow grade to the cantilevered bow of the bridge and still audible. When it crossed the bridge into Newport, I could hear it slow as it took the off ramp to head south on Highway 61. I knew there was a stoplight on 61, not far south of the bridge, and I could hear the truck ease to a halt. Then, when the light changed—this was well more than two miles away—I heard its acceleration.

I stood there listening to a truck fading somewhere into the highway system, like a radio signal sent out into the universe. And then I lost track, as the sound vanished into the evening and toward the far away.

## MOLLY RIVKIN

### *THE GIRL WITH UPSIDE DOWN EYES*

I watch the sky transform from pale gold to electric pink, then settle into a milky gray. A mass of clouds above the horizon's edge reflects the sun's descent. I sit in the snow, alone, and am cleared of any doubt I have been carrying. There is something so deeply honest about the sunset, something so deeply honest about Montana. Something pure. As I gaze at the slowly changing sky, other sunsets flash into my mind.

I am twenty-eight years old, standing alone in Regents Park in London, England. I have been here for an hour and the sun has started to set. I've been wandering a lot lately, picking up pigeon feathers, and trying to find meaning in the small patches of greenery amid a vast cityscape. I spend a lot of time sitting on park benches and staring at the sky, trying to silence my mind. I know I am deeper and vaster than my thoughts, but I am still searching for what that really means. So often the swirls and currents of passing thoughts carry me along and I am oblivious to my environment. I am seeking desperately. This is the second or maybe third time my mind has betrayed itself, and unraveled.

The first few times it was not shocking enough to change my personality too much. I have never been diagnosed with a mental health issue, but then again I have never spent too much time with a psychologist. I have been reasonably successful at any endeavor I have applied myself to but cannot deny my mind has edges. After tottering on those edges many times, I have recently taken a terrifying fall. Maybe we'll talk more about that later, maybe not. The point is, I am desperately seeking. I have started a hot yoga practice in a studio near Primrose Hill, a nice part of London.

That's where I live, with my haughty aunt. I have come to London to attain a master's degree in creative writing, specializing in spoken word poetry. A new and burning passion. I am doing well, despite the newness, strangeness, and courage it takes to share my heart in the form of spoken word poetry. Originally from a dysfunctional, but loving family in the rural mountains of northern Idaho, USA, I am not used to the cold aloofness of the city. My aunt's business-like approach to our relationship confuses me immensely. I had not yet learned detachment when I arrived in London, but certainly will by the time I depart.

We live in a large row house which my grandmother purchased in the 1960s for a reasonable price. Since her investment, the property value has sky-rocketed, and the neighborhood has become quite posh. My aunt's attitude has become quite posh with the neighborhood. I don't know how to relate. I have just finished a two-year Peace Corps stint in Ukraine, ending in a revolution and evacuation. I am very villagey in my demeanor and thinking. Posh doesn't make sense to me. I've been juggling so many different cultural identities. I am lost.

There is a lot more to the backstory and really the situation in general. Maybe we'll talk more about that later, but for now I am standing in Regents Park watching the most dazzling red sunset and singing softly to myself with a palm full of feathers. It's chilly. Damp, light mist, fall in London chilly. The trees on the other side of the football pitch look a bit like trees I've seen pictures of in the Sahara Desert. The deep red painted across the sky could be an African sunset if I forget the cold. I raise my voice a bit, a single note, not a song. Just sound evaporating into a rich and endless red. I sing until my voice is part of my body, and so I am real.

I sing until the light fades and the city sparkles around me. I am not a singer, but I do not care, this is not for anyone to hear, it is a gentle reminder that I have not disappeared. I feel weary as I walk back to my aunt's house. I hope she is asleep so I will not have to talk to her. I plan to go to yoga in the morning, and walk, and write and drink coffee. I plan to do everything in my power to stay alive another day. I am not sure why I have this tenacious instinct to cling to life. I am not sure why I am alive in the first place. The past couple of years have disconnected me from every relationship that has ever sustained me. Still, something in me begs to be kept alive, so I fight for that part every single day, and ignore the part that wants to die.

I live a privileged life. I know this. Even if it is held up by student loan debt. I have decided I am a writer and am in the process of creating that reality. I know how rare it is to have this opportunity and I remind myself daily, but I seem to have also acquired a writer's curse: a suicidal tendency and an unstable mind. I am not reckless with my body, I rarely get too drunk anymore, not after Ukraine. I don't take drugs. I eat well and exercise. Often, I feel quite healthy and joyous as well, but there is this part of my mind that prods at me. Maybe we will talk more about that later, I hope not.

Sometimes I think the sunset and early dark will last forever. The gray fading twilight hours linger on long after the disk of the sun has sunk below the flat endless horizon. I am sitting on a small metal deck that protrudes from an ancient and unused barn. The sky has become energetic orange fading up into a dusty yellow, then gray. When I stare long enough and hard enough, I forget about anything else. I forget how alone I feel here. I have been living in Ukraine for over a year, and this is the highest place I can find in the village. I like to get up high to have a look around. I think it has something to do with growing up in the mountains.

I am twenty-six years old. Peace Corps has always been a dream of mine. It was much more romantic in theory. In reality, I left America with a freshly broken heart. Though I have been learning so much here, and I am healing, I cannot call my existence joyful. I do have an abundance of time, that is a different experience. I am writing poetry. I am living the kind of life that demands poetry.

The bottom half of the sky is golden and magnificent over the swiftly passing corn fields. We are somewhere in Nebraska; we've been driving for hours. It's June and hot. I'm in the passenger seat and my best friend, Shaina, is driving. We've decided to road trip across America. Nothing makes sense anymore. We were evacuated from Ukraine about three months ago. We had served two years in our tiny villages before the Euromaidan Revolution, and Peace Corps evacuation. We have both managed to secure a summer job in Vermont with an international youth program. We have two weeks to get from Montana to Vermont in my shitty red Subaru. We're calling it the period wagon because we're both PMSing. After living abroad for such a long time, I have failed to mesh back into my north Idaho family culture. I don't know who I am anymore, and they don't either. I know I'm not ready to put my nose to the grindstone with all that intrinsic American work ethic. After Ukraine, I am looking for freedom.

I am twenty-seven years old. Shaina, and I just got tattoos. She's from

Texas and is too smart for her conservative southern culture. Now that we are back in America, we don't want to forget all the lessons we learned in Peace Corps. We don't want to forget how our world views unraveled, and how we are closer to truth than we have ever been. The tattoo is to remember, no matter where we are, we are free. A place has a way of shaping a person's thoughts, ours are still in Ukraine, we don't want America to restructure us again. We know it will. It's impossible to be immune from one's environmental influences.

We are camping next to the car most nights, sometimes we put the backseats down and both sleep in the car. First, we drive down to Utah to see the desert. Those vast open plains and spectacular mesa tops feel harsh after leaving the soft mountains of home. The car has been overheating sometimes, we can't figure out why. Took it to a mechanic in Salt Lake City, he couldn't figure it out either. As long as we are driving at highway speed everything is fine. We decide to drive as much as possible and hope for the best. Every time we stop for gas or food, we roll down the windows and blast the heat. We eat at roadside diners and fill the coolant tank. Sometimes there's a neon green coolant geyser if we don't let things cool down enough before checking the tank.

I brought some mushrooms. Shaina has never done hallucinogens and I think it's about time for her to try. We drive out into the Floy Wilderness to set up our tent and trip. Shaina doesn't like the feel of the place. Too far away, too secluded. The car has just overheated. Shaina is pissed, she isn't talking to me. We are out of cell service. We make a lunch of veggie wraps on top of the cooler. I decide to take a walk while Shaina and the car cool down.

It is deadly hot in the sun. I like the feeling of the dry heat inside my lungs. I am already sweating. On either side of me, huge red rock walls stretch toward the sky. The horizon is defined by cube-like rock structures. Small puffs of sage brush and desert foliage rise up on either side of me. The situation does seem precarious from an outsider's perspective, but I know it will be fine. It always is. Besides, we are in America now, everything is easier in America. At least we are fluent in the native language.

When I get back to the car, we put coolant in it, pack up and drive to the interstate. Shaina's mood lifts once we hit 80 miles per hour. We are headed to Colorado next to visit one of Shaina's lovers. She started using Tinder, a dating app, when she got back to the states. One of the guys she's been seeing moved to Aspen, Colorado. I think she is pretty ballsy to chase down a Tinder date. I don't mind being a third wheel, I have always wanted to see the Colorado mountains.

In my rearview mirror there is a symphony of color wedged between sloping mountains. It's the kind of pink that photos and paintings can't quite capture. There's something extradimensional about it, something you have to see with your eyes to understand.

I am thirty-one years old. I've been living in Missoula, Montana for three years. It's the longest I've ever lived anywhere since leaving my family home. Shaina is back in Texas, working with youth and immigrants. Doing good work. I am not. I am a whitewater raft guide, hungry for Montana's beauty and the chaos of the river. I feel most alive in the rapids, with the noise and uncertainty, with the energy of the water, the inevitable unpredictable motion. I am still not on a career path. I never have been. I am American again, indoctrinated again, part of a community again and happier than I have been in years.

The river has become my center, pulls like gravity. Life arranges itself around the river. A framework for everything else to fit into. When the fluctuations of the mind and heart leave me raw and wanting, the river is there moving, soothing, and flowing, calling me to her again and again. Alive and ever present, it's not about the men, or the friendships or the opinions of others. The river is always in motion, and I am in motion with her, belonging deeply. I grow to know her propensities, twists, turns, eddies, currents and swirls. An energy moves through her and ignites something in me, something whole and holy.

While guiding I learn the river's force can be lethal. There is no place for anything other than the task at hand. There can be no fighting against, instead the current must be ridden with trust, courage and ease. It is a deeply respectful partnership, river and guide, both know the river holds the power. Power of water surging onward, falling, cascading. The energy, the sound, the flow, tumbling toward its destiny. We are all tumbling toward our destinies. Truths, moments, lessons constantly revealing themselves. The ripple, the current, can't slow it down, move at its pace or it will drown you. The river arranges her shores into rock faces, exposed pastel colors displayed on towering surfaces. Teaches us vulnerability is beautiful. Teaches us, there's nothing wrong with turning inside out and showing what we are made of.

## ROBERT SPIEGEL

### *LAYERED IN SHADOW*

Do you know what sucks? When you get a good look into a different world. Like something moving in the corner of your eye. Then it suddenly comes full focus. And at first, you're not thinking this is a good thing. It changes you.

There's another world—and who knows how many more—layered and intertwined with this world. Once you see it, you can't unsee it. When you try to tell someone about it, they think you're full of shit. But you're not.

It doesn't come easy. You don't see this layered world until things break down in your life. For me, it began with a series of events that started with a goddamn fight with Mom. She thinks I'm not living up to my potential. She's right, but sometimes you don't know where to start to drag your life out of a ditch. She thinks she knows where I need to begin. That's the source of the fight. A fight is not such a big deal, except that this fight lasts day after day until I snap.

Every morning it starts with, "Where did you go last night."

"Out."

"Out where?"

"Out with friends."

"When did you get back?"

"I don't know."

"Well, I know. You got back at 5:00 in the morning."

That's followed by, "You can't lay around all day and go out god knows where all night long," until you say, "OK, I'm out of here."

Now what?

You wake up to the layered world slowly. Then all of a sudden. You're at the end of some rope. You don't know what you're going to do or where you're going to stay. You just know you had to get out of that house. You were dying there. But now you're starting to get hungry. Then some girl hanging out at Dylan's house says, "Want to take some acid?" You're not really sure, but she's pretty interesting and she seems to know what she's doing and you're completely lost, so shit.

"Stick out your tongue." You do, and she puts some small square of paper on your tongue and tells you to swallow it.

"Whole?"

"Yes, whole. Or chew it. Doesn't matter."

You do as she asks. Dylan says he has to go to work but it's all right if you stay. He says you can stay until you get on your feet. Huge relief. You're not sure what that means exactly, but you're thankful, and Dawn—she says that's not her real name but it's the name she likes—puts a piece of the acid paper in her mouth as well.

And you didn't realize how beautiful she was, and now you can see so clearly. She's wise and kind. Funny how the world begins to seem OK out of nowhere. You could follow her anywhere.

She tells you how this world isn't what you think it is. The world is fluid. It pours through us while we expand and contract. She's right. How did she know, and then she tells you about a world that lies alongside this world. You can feel it with parts of your mind. That's followed by parts of your body. You know exactly what she means.

※ ※ ※

The next morning you take a walk with Dawn. The bright summer sun is kind on your skin as you walk the dusty roads into town. Not far, about a mile. You're in this quiet Canadian town on Lake Huron, Kincardine, and it's Saturday morning and you hear the distant foghorns from the Great Lake boats and you can't remember how things got so screwed up with your mom. Dawn says, "Let's get breakfast."

You're standing in front of a bakery that has just opened. There's a sign in the window that says, "Help wanted." You get a box of tarts and doughnuts, a couple of cups of coffee, and you walk down to the rock garden where you sit on the bench eating this warm and delicious food as the boats go by in the foggy distance and you can see the old fisher guys at the end of the pier pulling up the occasional perch. And for the first time—maybe ever—the world is delicious like the tarts and the doughnuts.

A couple of mornings later you come by your mom's house—which so recently was your house—to get some clothes and things. Her eyes are puffy and red.

"So you decided to make an appearance."

You don't want to fight, and you know you don't have to.

"Sorry, Mom."

"Sorry?" Her eyes are not too puffy to show surprise.

"I've been shit. Sorry I've been shit. I need to get a few things. I won't be long."

Surprises keep coming over your mom's face, wave after wave.

"Where are you going? To your dad's?"

"I don't even know where Dad lives. I'm renting a room from Dylan."

"How are you going to pay for that? I suppose you need money." While she's breathing a bit easier now, she seems braced for a fight about money. She is fully committed to this world and almost certainly has no idea of other worlds.

"I got a job."

"Where?" A new wave of surprise. Something goes out of her like a balloon losing air. It's nice to see her face relax for the first time in probably your whole life.

"Bonnie's Bakery."

"Aunt Bonnie gave you a job?"

"Yeah, she was pretty happy about it. Said it's hard to find people you can trust. I guess she thinks she can trust me."

"She can. You and I have our fights, but she can trust you."

"We're not going to have fights anymore, Mom." I meant it. I had a new view of this world and its pathetic struggles.

She looked relieved and doubtful.

Why all the changes? When nothing matters, you can do anything. Not anything exactly, but you don't need to get upset about your mom, and you don't need to be so resistant to getting a job (which you wrongly expected would be rejection after rejection). Suddenly this world seemed less overwhelming because suddenly this world seemed smaller and less consequential. Don't know why you used to be so scared all the time. All you needed to do was ask for a job at a place that had a job offer in its window. And when I asked Dylan if I could rent a room, he was shocked. Someone was going to pay for some of his space. I told him I couldn't begin paying rent until I got paid and he said that was fine. I was amused to find this world isn't so hard when you know it doesn't have that much power. This world only thinks it can hurt you.

This world is crazy. It's missing a big part of itself. I learned that during the long night with Dawn, especially once she showed me the layered world.

One thing I learned is there's more than one me. And I learned that LSD is not like other drugs. Or at least the LSD that Dawn had. I used to think drugs were just for getting high. I sat in Dylan's living room with Dawn and she kept saying things like, "Do you see it now?"

"See what?"

"In front of you. That image, the shadowy one?"

"What?" I was confused. The acid was moving through me like electricity up and down my arms, up along my neck. Colors were becoming more intense. Even the white ceiling was turning a new white. I never realized white was a color.

"If you're willing to see it, there's an image of you. In front of you. Or maybe right within you. It's a bit different for each of us, each time."

"I don't know what you're talking about."

"Just stay with me here." She was quiet for a minute. Or maybe an hour.

"Your shadow is right here. It's the rest of you. Without it, you're lost. Mostly you've been lost. But there was a time you were not lost."

Sitting on that couch in Dylan's living room, I didn't feel high. I felt different. I had no idea what she was talking about, but she was right. I had been lost—all my life—or at least since I was a little kid. She stayed quiet, occasionally saying, "It's right there. If you find it, you'll never be lost again. It's you. It's nobody but you."

She took some records out and started playing that quiet music that's not like music at all. She just let me sit there in those weird thoughts, feeling strange. Sometimes I'd forget to breathe, and then I'd remember and start breathing again.

Dawn was beautiful, like a sister, though I didn't have a sister. Not like a cute girl. I don't know what she was like. But everything I was angry about—I don't even know everything I was angry about—was all dripping out of me. I thought I was mad at Mom. That wasn't it; it wasn't even Dad, wherever he was. Anger was dripping out of me, I don't know what it was except some kind of rattlesnake poison that was leaving my body, oozing out of some small holes in my skin that hurt like cuts. The pain from the cuts felt so much easier than the pressure of holding in all of the purple-black rages.

The night lasted forever. The room seemed tiny, and then it seemed huge. The colors of everything, my pants, Dawn's hair, her face, were colors I hadn't seen before. I was thinking they might be new to the world, but that doesn't sound right.

Every once in a while I'd ask Dawn if I was OK. And she'd say, "You're beautiful." I didn't believe that, but it was nice to hear.

Sometime in the middle of that long night, Dawn said, "Do you see it?" I still didn't know what she was talking about. We seemed to be somewhere else even though I recognized the living room.

"It shifted. We crossed." What? I looked at my hand and it wasn't my hand. She was whispering, "It's OK. It's OK. Just follow me. We're out in a field." I knew we weren't out in a field, but it made so much sense just to follow her words. "You've been here before," and by golly she was right. And we were still in the living room. "This is where you find yourself. You're not troubled here."

She was talking slowly. Not pushing for me to understand. Just letting me slowly get it. "You're shadow's right here. Right with you. There is kindness here. There is a flow of mercy." And I felt it. And it wasn't a hallucination. We were still in the living room, but we were somewhere gentle. And I felt whole. I felt completely whole. Like the days when I was a kid out in the woods and I was part of the pond and the field and the trees and the frogs.

⚜ ⚜ ⚜

During the next few days, when I would see Dawn, she would smile at me in a certain knowing way, and someplace deep inside me welled up with a sense of love. That day, the morning after the night with Dawn, when we were sitting in the rock garden watching the distant boats go by, she explained that it wasn't the acid.

"What wasn't the acid?"

"That place you got to last night." She could see I was pretending to be normal. She laughed. "OK, whatever."

I snapped out of my phony indifference—an old habit. "OK, OK, I know what you mean. I won't pretend I don't."

"The acid helped. It opened the door. But the place you got to was you."

I laughed. "It wasn't me. I don't think I had anything to do with it. You did it. I just followed."

"You were willing."

"So what now? More acid? Acid every week like church?"

"You don't ever have to take acid again. Acid is not usually the best tool, even though it worked last night. You're right to ask 'what now.' Your sense of not being split, not being broken will fade." She sighed lightly. "The rock garden is so cool."

"Where are you from?"

"Nova Scotia. Seattle. By way of Ohio. It doesn't matter where I'm from."

"Did you go through this with Dylan?"

"He was my little brother's best friend growing up. I decided to stop by on my way to Vancouver."

"Did you?"

"Dylan and I did acid some time ago. He liked it OK. But no. He just got high. He learned a little. He didn't want to do much work. He wasn't in trouble. He admitted that he thought my ideas were kinda full of shit. He told me that in a nice way."

The light layer of fog began to lift, leaving behind small waves twinkling in the sun. I watched one of the fisher guys pull up a small perch. He looked at it, shrugged, and threw it back

"The shadow moved into me."

"I know it did. Now you have to figure out what to do with the rest of your life."

"Yes, I kinda do."

"You're not angry anymore."

"I'm not. How'd you know I was angry."

She looked at me and smirked. "Really?"

How do you live your life? Where do you go from here? Nowhere. Everywhere. What's life like when everything is different and you never get

back to where you were?

I worked at Bonnie's. I lived at Dylan's. Every Sunday, I went over to Mom's for dinner. We didn't have anything to fight about. I could see how lovely she was. I could see how much she loved me. More than she knew.

I started going to Fanshawe College in Goderich and later on, I finished my bachelor's at Western University sixty miles east in London. Then on to graduate work in Toronto. I opened a bakery in London, and later in Toronto when I moved there. I became a psychologist. Me. Stupid me. Believe it or not, I took up shadow studies. Can you imagine you can actually study the shadow self? It's an edgy-yet-legitimate side of psychology. But all that's on the side. My real interest is this other world that resides right here. I don't know much about it, but it was the home of the shadow I found with Dawn, and I know it's a world of love. I can see it. Every day. Always. Right here. In front of me. In me. Stupid, huh?

I see Dawn every couple of years. She wanders like a gypsy. Vancouver to Los Angeles, to Santa Fe, a couple of years in Sedona. She does seminars, retreats, podcasts, church talks, an ever-present blog, and even a book. I taught her book when I finally had my class on the shadow self at the University of Toronto. I'd ask how it was going with her work helping people find their shadows.

She'd shrug. "It's my work."

"Are you getting anywhere? I have some shadow-work clients, but I only get so far. Of course, I don't use LSD."

"I haven't used LSD in decades. I get somewhere with each student, clients if you will. I get somewhere. It's important to work even if success is limited."

"Do you ever get all the way with any of your clients?"

"I did once. One time. Hell, maybe that's enough."

"And how did it go with that person?"

She looked at me and smirked. "Really?"

# SIDNEY STEVENS

## *TWO-MINUTE WARNING*

Here's what I know is true.

Stephen lies beside me in the semi-darkness of another chill spring morning, breathing lightly in sleep as he often does this time of day. He's warm beside me and restless, almost awake. I can't imagine lying next to anyone else now. He groans softly and rolls over, keeping perfectly to his side of the bed in the dip he's created over time. I know the full feel of him there, neatly furrowed in the folds of our mattress and my brain after nearly twenty years together.

The alarm will ring soon. We'll both rise, he first into the shower and I right after. Neither of us eats breakfast, possibly a holdover from our graduate school days when we were always running off to the next thing. And possibly because we don't have kids and never fell into a family routine. I didn't want them and still don't feel the call. Stephen did for years. He used to bring it up often, or stop to linger at the ballpark where Little League teams play in the evenings. I hate keeping him from fatherhood, but I can't make myself want what I don't. He could've left me any time for someone more maternal. But he hasn't. He rarely brings it up now. He's given up asking me to marry him, too.

Stephen will walk down the stone path out back to the 1930s garage he's converted into a small studio with skylights and lots of plants. I like his studio as much as he does, but I rarely wander out there. Better to not disturb all those blueprints and sketches piled around him. It's the one realm he inhabits without me.

Stephen is an architect, specializing in energy-efficient buildings with solar panels, bamboo floors, and cellulose insulation made from recycled denim. A majority of his clients here in southeast Pennsylvania don't seek eco-friendly design, so Stephen churns out mostly uninspired cookie-cutter mega-homes in treeless cornfield developments with stone veneer siding and vaulted ceilings. I know he'd give his right arm, and left one too, to design wild, giant, undulating museums, skyscrapers and eternal monuments. But that's not happened for him.

I taught urban planning at Gunther College in town for a three years as an adjunct professor. I'd hoped for a full-time faculty job, but it never materialized, even after I promised to finish my PhD. I now substitute-teach in the public schools and handle publicity for a small downtown art gallery housed in a converted silk mill with exposed brick walls and floor-to-ceiling windows. I also try to work on my book every day, an offshoot of my doctoral thesis on innovative ways cities and towns are preparing for climate change. I adore the topic, but the writing is slow.

Stephen will trudge back to the house about six, unless he's meeting a client. He's usually rumpled looking and tired. So am I. Most nights we cook together, side by side in our crowded kitchen, typically vegetarian stews and stir-fries interspersed with an occasional steak or salmon. Sometimes we go out to eat, sticking with one of the trendy restaurants that line the charming streets of our town's revitalized historic district. Or we dine with friends. On Saturday we'll bike along the Delaware Canal if it doesn't rain. Last weekend we ventured into New York for a tour of the New Museum of Contemporary Art, including an outside exploration of the building itself (for Stephen), which was designed to look like a massive pile of irregularly stacked boxes. Last summer we traveled to France and Germany. This summer a big trip looks doubtful because I had fewer teaching jobs and Stephen's client base shrank. There's always next year. I currently feel a pull toward Argentina or Thailand. Stephen isn't so keen on either, but will go if I plead enough.

It's a good life. For the most part, Stephen and I feel fulfilled and motivated, partaking in personal and professional activities we enjoy and hopefully contributing something to the world.

Here's what's also true.

What I've just described is the story I tell myself and others. It's what anyone would see upon the closest scrutiny of our lives. I fully embrace this narrative—on the surface it's absolutely true. Until some buried urge pushes up, despite my best efforts to keep it hidden, reminding me that this account doesn't fully flesh out the tale.

No one can see what I hide as I write multiplication problems on the blackboard or empty my grocery cart at the checkout line, how my nerve endings are often numb, synapses in my brain on half speed. How many days I go through the motions, laughing on cue with the other teachers on break, reaching for another plate to wash in the kitchen sink, nuzzling against Stephen as I chop onions and he sautés mushrooms, pecking out words on my laptop that don't seem to capture everything I want to say. I live these moments physically, but not in some deeper way where they might actually count or archive into memory. I only do them because I must for day-to-day life to function.

It occurs to me increasingly that maybe I haven't felt the fullness of anything for more years than I care to count.

I'm not depressed. I've been down that road before, where everything worth having, like joy and love and the burst of rich red flavor from fresh-picked strawberries seems permanently and hopelessly locked behind tinted, murky glass. Things right now don't look muddied or muffled so much as just an inch removed from reach, running closely parallel but not quite close enough to access the full experience.

I hammer myself for offering such a cliché. My life is plentiful with what anyone would want. Who doesn't occasionally feel numb? I love Stephen. I do. Many days I feel truly fortunate. Yet more and more during odd, quiet moments—while paying bills, scrubbing toilets, or even as Stephen and I wander our neighborhood on lovely summer evenings, down tree-lined streets, past well-maintained mature homes, hand in hand, kids whizzing by on bikes, shouting across yards and lots—I'm increasingly certain I should have kept exploring other paths instead of rejecting them outright.

Here's what could have been true.

For the record let me say this: I'm a better person than I was before Stephen. That I know for a fact. Maybe it's his steady, kind influence. Living with anyone rubs off the pointy edges, but Stephen's thoughtful, sweet disposition has rubbed off way more edges than I thought possible (he never fails to massage my feet after long teaching days and lets me vent as much as needed when I get stressed, always with a patient smile). I'm kinder and more aware of others because of him, more willing to create space for them and their wishes, more inclined to yield my space in line to a senior or giggle with toddlers. It's sincere, too. I'm also more confident, more settled, more certain about what makes me happy and what doesn't.

With Anthony I was the mirror opposite—like dwelling on the black side of a yin-yang symbol. I was more fearful, more haunted by a sense of darkness that has tinted my thoughts from earliest memory. Which should make me happy that I now live on the lighter side with Stephen.

And yet that old pre-Stephen darkness has begun showing up again with rising regularity. I'm pulled to re-examine a past I once fled—my mom's stifling MS and my dad's stifling devotion to her care, the suffocation and tedium they both endured, and still do, never generating quite enough concern for me or my brother. I thought I'd put those memories away for good.

I replay my life with Anthony again and again, too, the life I ultimately didn't pursue, his desire to travel every inch of the planet, sample every human being in his path—young and old, good and bad, every shape and size—each one fodder for his fascination. I met him after college as I roamed the country in search of me. I found him instead, sleeping in a ragged tent outside Sebastopol, California instead of his parents' Connecticut estate, train-hopping and hitchhiking from town to town, bathing in rivers and bus stations, foraging in gardens at night and in stinky dumpsters. I joined him without hesitation to explore America, then Asia and Europe—forever ignoring his disregard for my deepest being, his inability to love anyone.

I wasn't as nice with Anthony. I was more like him, lashing out with ugly words and put-downs when I felt most vulnerable, self-absorbed and near narcissism in my pursuit of things and experiences to make me happy. I finally released it all into a different kind of life.

I left Anthony on a cloudy morning in Barcelona, and my parents before that, and a thousand other possible lives because they dredged up dysfunction and pain I decided to escape. I enrolled in grad school, met Stephen while filling out forms at orientation (I asked to borrow his pen), and have labored these years to bury my unpleasant past in work, relationships and good deeds, behind smiles and pleasing gestures—cookies for neighbors, phone calls to sick friends, charitable contributions to causes that move me.

I believed my escape was successful. And yet suddenly I can't seem to paper over the darkness, which is darker now and more alive than back then. I find myself screaming along with rage songs as I drive alone down tame suburban streets, howling anguished lyrics with a satisfying fury I've never let myself fully feel. I crave piercings and bomb explosions and the emptiness of lonely roads.

I can hardly bear to contemplate what's suddenly all too clear: my life is ordinary. A loaded word, I know. Ordinary is subjective. But let's just say I'm not exactly who I meant to be, close perhaps, but a lackluster version. I ache to torch what's *respectable*, smash its nice doodads and pleasantries to bits, speed away and never return.

Apparently, I didn't morph into a sunnier, happier me with Stephen after all. I simply disowned my darkness to the point of numbness, becoming less than fully resplendent. Because to segregate darkness from the entire emotional mix and bury it alone is impossible. Pain simply can't be untangled from the whole and anesthetized without deadening all other feelings with it, including the good.

When I was with Anthony, I wished like hell not to stand out. I thought darkness tinged my flesh, like black jaundice. Now that I'm away from that step outside the line, I wish like hell to kick ass again.

Here's what I've decided to make true.

The plan, the urge, is an old one, always shoved aside before it reaches real awareness. Suddenly it's recognizable enough for execution. I've decided to leave Stephen.

I decided this morning as he yawned in the bathroom, louder than necessary and ending in a grating grunt.

I decided as he shuffled to the shower, leaving behind an aroma mix of yesterday's faded cologne and something akin to raw eggs. I decided when he kissed the top of my head before strolling to his office and murmured, "So long, Midge," (his nickname for me since the beginning, a play on my given name, Margaret), as though it's still as clever and fresh as it seemed then.

I decided last week when I noticed I can't see as well as last year. I need new glasses. I decided while recharging my phone halfway through yesterday after having already recharged it once before breakfast. I need a new phone. I decided when I couldn't retrieve a synonym for *livelihood* or *expansion* as I squirmed at my laptop last week to work on my book after school in the dingy teacher's lounge. I decided while observing the flabbiness of my upper arms through a dull ache behind my right eye as the janitor wheeled his clattery cart down the empty hall.

What would life even look like without Stephen? Nothing ever comes to mind. Unimaginable. My life with him is an integral part of my world. He is half my days and nights. I can't imagine losing the security of his familiar face, lopsided jaw and green eyes behind rimless glasses. But last summer when he glanced at me on a hot, Philadelphia street munching a mouthful of pierogies and I saw only his slackening jowl, a certain stiffening of his preferences (he only chooses cheese pierogies now instead of the variety he once preferred), his quiet nature turned even quieter over time with longer and longer stretches of wordlessness, I knew I couldn't pretend waning love isn't a possibility.

The overwhelming urge to leave today feels like the only right thing to do. Stephen and I—so comfortable together for so long—may in fact be losing the gravitational force that's held us steady all these years. I doubt he's noticed, but it's beyond clear to me. Did I slide into orbit around Stephen based on who I was when we met instead of who I hoped to become, someone I'm now becoming?

Here's what's true that I didn't know until today.

In between tucking athletic socks into my suitcase this morning and selecting knickknacks and mementos to take with me, I made a discovery quite by accident—call it an ineradicable second look.

Analogies don't do it justice, but it was akin to staring at an old photo of yourself from a time when you despised some feature of your appearance. You can remember the general scorn you felt for the shape of your legs or the breadth of your nose or whatever trait you detested—a flaw so monstrous as to overshadow everything else. And yet as you view the photo now there's hardly a hint of that fatal flaw. You were lovely and fresh and deliciously young. The perceived defect is barely noticeable. So much irretrievable time lost not loving yourself, wishing you were beautiful, and come to find out you were all along.

The most striking thing: Nothing about your flaw has actually changed in physical reality. It's merely a shift in perception, nudged along by time. And that's where the analogy diverges, for my ability to perceive things anew this morning required almost no passage of years. I simply glanced out our bedroom window at a snapshot of my life and it magically rearranged itself in a matter of moments.

There was Stephen in his rattiest jeans, the ones I hate most, heading to his office in the morning sunshine. I noticed a shuffle in his walk, a slight lean to the left that I don't remember when he was younger, and a rigidity about his shoulders, a thinning of his his salt-and-pepper waves, which used to be fuller and wavier when his hair was darker. There was a noticeable crack in the foundation of his office building that I also don't remember, and a seedling growing from the gutters we never clean. Our bedroom felt cramped. Dust had collected on the sunny windowsill around last year's withered amaryllis. The coffee I drank earlier churned uncomfortably in my stomach, a new brand with a pleasing leaf-covered label that tasted weak.

An ancient ache erupted inside me, wave after awful wave, like being gutted alive. Life was supposed to be so much more than this. I wanted a stunning man, wildly successful, world renowned, brilliant. All those things. I wanted passionate love with him to last a lifetime. I never wanted a mansion, but I did want land, acres and acres all my own, and a giant old house that we'd restore with outbuildings and stately trees. I wanted to be world-renowned too—a paradigm-shifting visionary of sustainable living—with luxury to pursue a totally private life on my own terms. I wanted enough money to explore ten thousand places, climb mountains, hike rain forests, sleep in luxury hotels under satin sheets and on white beaches. I wanted things to look more perfect, feel more perfect, smell and taste and sound more perfect. I wanted to feel alive and thrilled and productive every moment of every day. I wanted an exceptional life.

Then abruptly what I just described as intolerably insufficient—this snapshot of my life—transformed in a flash from stunning imperfection to its opposite extreme, sweeping through every sense organ from some deeper inner organ of knowing lodged well below the chaos of life's habitual dissatisfactions and hungers. The sorry details of my life spontaneously mutated into a swirl of darling treasures, reconfiguring without fanfare but with vigorous, decisive efficiency, like an impartial electronic data dump. Somehow I could unravel gigabytes of insight instantaneously and grasp it all perfectly.

I found myself fully enfolded and loved in the center of life as never before, absorbing the warm goo and vibrant colors, breathing in the scent of soil and pollen, listening to birds and wind, feeling the pain I've known— darkness and disappointment and loss—as well as all the happiness and wonders, too. I felt it all, full to the brim, for the first time in my life, and my heart cracked wide open for Stephen and me, his sagging jeans, his lack of big commissions, my lack of publishing credits, the gray-green paint on our bedroom walls that I've never liked and the red oak stain on our living room floor that's too dark, and our nest egg which isn't yet sufficient to retire on.

I saw a million things not to love, but I loved them all in that moment. A miracle of the universal game clock—a do-or-die moment of reflection with only two minutes left to play.

So profound was this love the only thing I could do was quietly empty my suitcase, set knickknacks and mementos back on tables and shelves, grab my purse and briefcase and back down the driveway for work. Just like any other day. Except that old thoughts about what form life must take to make me happy had dimmed beneath a new overlay of alternative thoughts. I realized I can think them instead. My dreams don't have to come true. They are made up after all from another life. I can make up new ones for this life, rotate my mind a notch to harness deeper joys. Joy is here already—more than enough. I can work with what I have and who I am.

Now, as I drive past our bank and Stephen's favorite sushi restaurant, Toshi, I marvel at the bright April sun illuminating everything in crisp shadows and supernaturally vivid colors—tree blossoms, road signs, neckties and cars alike. I continue up Belmont Street to Baker Elementary School, slip into the building through a rear door and move down the cool, unlit hallway toward Room 304 where this week I'm teaching fifth grade. I plop at my desk, students not yet here, and surrender again to stillness. Beautiful stillness. I've fallen in love with what is just in time not to lose it.

Faraway footsteps and voices echo down the hall as students enter the building, pulling me back toward the surface. Agitation ripples there, nervous energy. A student shuffles into the room past my desk to her seat. A sliver of sunlight slanting through the window shimmers a little less than earlier. Another student arrives and another. The shimmer fades more. A text from Stephen reminds me to pick up asparagus for dinner. I delete it with an impatient jab—he's already reminded me twice. Was it all just a blip of imagination? A passing epiphany?

I plummet back to class with a thud. Bored faces watch me watching them. Epiphanies come and go, yet the essence of what's true lingers: I've seen a deeper place where I can burrow as needed for quiet counsel and healing, to explore myself and life with Stephen, make needed tweaks without human blinders and fear, with the whole of my being, using the eyes of my heart. That's where happiness lies, waiting to be carried out to my world, not the other way around. If only I remember the way, still raw-cut through my mind, barely perceptible beneath surface turbulence and the mesmerizing pull of other pastures. If only I remember—moment by moment, day by day, through all of life.

# SHERRY SHAHAN

## *LOITERING*

I am four years old. Sitting on the edge of the porcelain tub while my mother paints on her cat-eyes.

It is not enough to watch her in the reflection of the tri-fold mirror. I want her to face me, to feel her arms around me, to squeeze me until bedtime. Instead, she sprays her sweeping up-do with Aqua Net.

Eight years old.
I still wait.

Now I want to tell you about my mother's rabbit. It died when she was sixteen. But that's a misnomer since all rabbits tested died. A few days after being injected, the female is sliced open. Ovaries change in response to hormones secreted by a pregnant human.

Twelve years old. I have stopped waiting.
But I want my mother to tell me the lie that everything will be okay.

I am seventeen. My rabbit dies.
My mother's tears gather on her cheeks.

I am thirty-two. My mother and I come together over the evening news and a cocktail, adult conversations, book-ended with laughter—returning to the same stories, family history relived, reorganized, rewritten.

In the memory, she smiles at me. This is why the memory sticks.

Let me tell you about the first day of spring eight years ago? When sunlight reminds me of children reciting a nursery rhyme.

My mother lounges on the loveseat beneath the living room window. She chose the plaid fabric from Sears, her favorite go-to department store. She is hooked to an oxygen tank, shrunken inside her fake-velvet jogging suit, her cat-eyes deep in a trashy paperback, living her last moments like clouds in an ever changing sky.

I am in my sixties, standing in the driveway of my mother's home of sixty-four years. My mother's beloved lemon tree is lifeless. Her clay pots, cracked, shriveled roots exposed. No bees or butterflies.

Her hushed voice presses the silence. *Does any part of us remain here? Does a house begin to settle in on itself when abandoned? Is it the breath of the occupants that hold it up?*

But first I want to tell you about my stepfather of forty years. Lost. Lonely. Vulnerable.

The family fears he has become a host to a parasite who has oddly become executor of the estate and co-signer on bank and retirement accounts. The parasite buys a $90,000 Tesla, registered solely in his name.

While hosting this organism my father loses fifty pounds and dies alone on an autumn day when every branch is leafless.

The parasite drives away.

I want to tell you about the house, empty, the air stale, unable to exhale. A door slams for no reason.

There are alternatives to what I am doing. They just do not interest me.

The parasite nailed a second curtain rod above the front window and hung a thick red blanket; a veil of dull dust, deception and danger.

I climb onto the loveseat in a crossroad of time, sorrow quivering through my bones, and lift the curtain rod from its bracket. Afternoon light bores through the window in flaxen triangles. I am reminded that this is the only time of year when sun touches the deepest crannies of the living room.

I sit on the brick patio under my mother's orange tree, planted so she could bag fruit for family and friends. Because this tree is alive with blossoms I stretch my fingers and keep stretching them, knowing healing begins on the uppermost branch.

# MURALI KAMMA

## *LEARNING THE GAME*

Opening the creaky door to enter the lobby, Hari was so surprised to see him—an older white man, walking briskly in his direction—that he stared, without meaning to, before smiling in embarrassment when the man said hello. Dressed in a plaid blue flannel shirt and tan cargo pants, he seemed to be in his late seventies. His wispy, unruly white hair, a little long, stuck out on the sides, and he wore rimless glasses and a gray beret, giving him a vaguely bohemian look. Perhaps the beret covered a bald patch, Hari thought, as he returned his greeting and kept the door open, waiting until the man, thanking him politely, exited the building.

The frayed carpet gave off a faint musty odor, which mingled with cooking smells, as Hari passed the elevator—now working, unlike last time—and climbed the stairs, two at a time, till he reached the third floor. The aging, graffiti-scarred building had seen better days, and the protruding window air-conditioners, for those apartments that had them, made it clear that a renovation was long overdue. Stopping at the second door, he knocked.

Hari wondered why he'd reacted in that cringe-inducing manner when he saw the man in the lobby. The sitcom he'd begun writing, albeit only in his head and when he needed a diversion, was taking an unexpected turn. So far, the only characters to make an appearance were immigrants and refugees who lived in this building. For the opening shot, Hari had envisioned a bunch of residents in front of the building. But since none of them were white, here was a twist to throw viewers off and make the beginning more intriguing. What was this older gentleman doing in a building filled with foreign-born people who were younger and didn't look like him?

On Hari's previous visits, he'd only seen people of color, almost all of whom were recent refugees and immigrants. Was the man a visitor, like Hari? Possibly. More likely, he lived in the building—and his presence, announced so early, added to the drama forming in Hari's head.

Hari's real-life job was more mundane, though he liked it. A staff correspondent for Diaspora Weekly, he was currently working on a feature article about refugees and other recent immigrants in the neighborhood. How did the two communities get along, and what sort of challenges did they face while adapting to their new lives in America? Having already talked to a bunch of people, he was now returning for one of his last interviews. The door opened to reveal Abdul. A slightly built man with a gentle manner and a receding hairline, he welcomed Hari with a smile and introduced him to his wife, Nilofar, who was in the living room close by.

After the interview was over, as Hari put away his recorder, Nilofar brought cups of tea and Parle-G biscuits from the kitchen. Sipping the soothing, fragrant beverage, Hari casually mentioned the man he'd seen in the lobby. Yes, they knew him but not very well, Abdul said. He came to the nearby park to watch the residents play cricket.

"Cricket?" Hari looked up from his cup, wondering if he'd heard correctly.

Abdul laughed. "Yes. His name is Morris. For a long time, he was confused by the rules. But he still comes, to watch and chat with the players. He likes the game now."

While Abdul, who was less outgoing than the cricket players, didn't know him as well as they did, the old man was friendly, he said, if a little eccentric.

"How so?"

"Well, he's the only American here . . . I should say white American. I don't ever see him with other whites who are family or friends."

Hari was baffled by this reasoning, but instead of questioning Abdul further, he thanked him and Nilofar for their time and hospitality, and said he'd be back in a couple of days.

Reaching the main street, after walking along a cracked sidewalk flanked by uncut weeds, Hari saw a food cart, parked strategically close to a metro bus stop. The rain had left puddles of muddy water, which pedestrians had to watch because of passing vehicles. A commercial strip on the other side of the street had a grocery store, a couple of ethnic restaurants, a thrift store, and a hair salon. From the food cart, Hari bought a bottle of water and a falafel wrap garnished with onions and peppers and squirts of white and red sauce.

Then he headed to the park. Not many people were around at this time, as far as Hari could tell, but he was impressed by the park's size. Gentrification hadn't arrived here, saving this vast expanse of grassy land—it didn't look like a typical park—from marauding developers. Walking along an uneven dirt path, Hari looked for a place to sit and have his lunch.

Hari spotted a bench, but then stopped in shock before he got too close. It was occupied by the man he'd seen in the lobby. With his eyes closed, and interlocked hands resting on a gently heaving chest, he seemed to be meditating or sleeping. Hari turned around and started walking away, but then stopped again when he heard the man's voice.

"Hi there. You're welcome to join me. There's enough space here."

Walking up to the bench, Hari said, "I didn't want to bother you. I was just going to have my lunch."

"No bother at all," he said, moving a little to make more space. "Please sit. I wasn't sleeping. Didn't I see you earlier?"

"Indeed. You were leaving the apartment building just as I was going in."

"Yes, of course. I'm Morris, by the way."

"Hari. Pleased to meet you. Have you had your lunch?"

"Oh, don't mind me," Morris said. "I'm fasting. The food truck's falafel wrap is delicious, but it doesn't tempt me now." He laughed. "I'll have a light meal this evening."

"How often do you fast?"

"Once a week, on the day I'm not working. Are you a reporter?"

Stunned, Hari looked at him, though he finished chewing before he spoke. "Yes, I work for Diaspora Weekly. How did you know?"

"Just guessed. I've seen your paper. I enjoyed going through it on a few occasions."

"Thank you. I'm wondering where you came across it."

"In the building," Morris said. "I'm a resident there, and I saw your paper in another guy's apartment. He organizes cricket matches."

"So, you like cricket? It's been many years since I played it. I used to love the game."

"I found it confusing for a long time." Morris chuckled. "But I'm much better now."

Having finished eating, Hari put away his water bottle. "Have you lived here for a while?" he asked, turning to face him.

"In the building, you mean? This is my fourth year here as a tenant. Before that I did live in this area, though it was almost three decades ago."

"Things must have changed since then," Hari said.

"Sure. Saying that it was different then is an understatement. Looking back, I realize that I was part of the flight. I'd have disagreed if somebody had said that. My decision, I'd have argued, was unrelated to what others around me were doing. But now I can see that it was an accurate tag for what happened. After all, sociologists have studied it."

Hari looked at him in puzzlement.

"White flight," Morris said, and chuckled again. "I was part of the exodus."

"I see." Feeling awkward because he couldn't think of an adequate response, Hari looked up as a flock of birds, chattering agitatedly, glided downward like planes making an emergency landing. Then Hari added, "I once saw some old pictures of this neighborhood. It was much greener back then . . . seemed more like farmland. Well, it's time to get back to my office."

"Sure. See you around."

※ ※ ※

Two days later, Hari was back at the apartment building. Abdul had offered to introduce him to another tenant for Hari's final interview.

It was a crisp fall day, with an energizing nip in the air, when Hari entered the lobby again and, skipping the stairs this time, took the aging elevator—noisy and a little wobbly—up to the third floor. The apartment building appeared to be quieter than usual. While the opening scene of Hari's sitcom had felt promising, now it wasn't going anywhere. He couldn't think of any clever lines, scenes, jokes. His imagination had hit a roadblock, making him realize how hard it was to write fiction, even sitcom-style fiction. Creating zany characters and twisty plots was not his forte. But there was nonfiction, thankfully, and his job allowed him to tell newsy community-oriented stories that, he hoped, engaged the weekly's readers.

Nilofar was at work, but Abdul's friend Kapil, who lived on another floor, greeted Hari with a vigorous handshake. Well built, especially in comparison to Abdul, Kapil had the lithe bearing of an athlete—and his complexion, a deeper brown, seemed at least partly linked to the time he apparently spent in outdoor pursuits.

"It's Kapil who organizes our cricket matches," Abdul said. "Please sit and start the discussion. I'll make some tea."

Hari offered to take them to lunch, but both Abdul and Kapil said that another day would be better. Settling back in his chair, Hari said he hadn't played cricket in ages.

Smiling broadly, Kapil said, "Well, if you're interested, you can come anytime to our practice sessions in the park here. I can share our schedule."

Taking his card, Hari thanked him and noted that he was more of a spectator these days.

Saying that spectators were also welcome, Kapil elaborated on what was clearly a big passion. He talked about how cricket, ignored or virtually unknown in mainstream America, had gained a foothold in certain immigrant communities. The neighborhood, he said, had a full-fledged cricket team that had many players from their apartment building. Although Kapil didn't say so, Hari realized he was the main organizer of the matches played in the park.

"I heard about the matches," Hari said. "A couple of days ago, I met Morris in the park. He told me about them . . . I believe he mentioned you, though not by name."

"You met Morris? Wonderful. I know him very well. Yes, he comes to watch our matches." Grinning, Kapil added, "At first he used to find the game confusing, even tedious. Now he's much better. He enjoys the game, or at least I think he does."

"We had a nice but brief chat. I guess he's retired."

"No, he still works at the thrift store. I've seen him there."

Hari didn't say anything, though he was taken aback. Morris didn't look like somebody who worked at a thrift store. What was his job there? Hari was even more astonished by what Kapil said next. Earlier, Morris used to work at a retail company's huge warehouse, where employees processed online orders of merchandise for immediate shipment. The pace was so grueling that Morris, who had felt like a tightly controlled robot, quit his job after a few months and opted for a less stressful position at the thrift store, where he was paid by the hour.

Although Hari remained silent, he realized that Kapil was aware of his revelation's impact. "The financial meltdown we had was a big setback for Morris, as it was for many others," he continued, accepting a cup of tea from Abdul.

"Morris and his wife had a nice house and everything," Abdul added, after handing another cup to Hari. Holding the third cup, he sat next to Hari on the worn purple sofa.

"Indeed," Kapil said. "I drove by it once. It's in an upscale neighborhood.

But they lost everything, and then they got divorced."

"Any children?" Hari asked, putting his cup down on the wobbly, oval-shaped wooden coffee table after taking a long sip.

"Two stepchildren, I believe, though I've never seen them," Kapil said. "Morris was an executive when they were living in that house. When the company he was at got bought out, he took a severance package. He has always had an interest in sports, and he saw that as an opportunity to become an entrepreneur."

"Doing what?" Hari asked.

"I don't know all the details, honestly, and I didn't want to probe him," Kapil said. "I know they started an academy that combined his passion for sports with education. He had a partner who was experienced in these matters, but unfortunately it didn't go far."

"Yes, the timing was bad," Abdul chimed in. "The idea was to facilitate the coaching of deserving children in various sports. But the idea fell apart, and they lost a lot of money."

"So, he didn't try to go back to what he was doing before?" Hari said.

"No," Kapil said. "It's complicated. There was financial impropriety, and the lenders weren't happy. It seems to have been the partner's fault . . . I'm not sure what actually happened. I do know that only the partner went to prison. Here's what I believe: Morris was a victim. Not only did he suffer financially but his reputation was damaged." Kapil paused, before adding, "Shall we start the interview? As I mentioned, my shift begins at 2 p.m."

"Of course," Hari said, reaching for his recorder. "It shouldn't take long."

After Hari finished asking his questions, he thanked Kapil and promised to be in touch again to let them know when the article would appear in Diaspora Weekly.

"Please come this Saturday if you can spare some time," Kapil said as they shook hands. "We're playing the season's first cricket match. The other team is good, really good. But if I may say so, our team is better." He laughed. "It should be worth watching."

"I would love to," Hari said. "It's been ages since I watched a live cricket match."

Arriving at the park on Saturday morning, Hari was again impressed by its size. Walking farther this time, he came to the open space where the cricket match was already in progress. A large crowd had gathered, and the mood was festive. There was a loud thwack, to the accompaniment of cheers, as Hari watched a batsman punch the red ball for a stylish cover drive. A fielder raced to retrieve it, but not before the batsmen exchanged places for a run. The ball was being thrown back to the bowler when Hari heard a familiar voice. It was Abdul, calling out excitedly from the stands. Hari made his way toward him through the crowd.

"The other side is batting, but we're doing well," Abdul said, shifting to make room for Hari next to him. "We already picked up four wickets." Smiling, he added, "Kapil is in the front row, close to the action. He's a coach these days, more than a player."

The fielders, fanned out on the ground, had canary yellow T-shirts, while the two batsmen, standing at opposite ends of the pitch, were wearing sky blue T-shirts. The atmosphere was joyful but tense, and Hari could tell that the spectators were quite involved in the game. Some were sharing snacks or taking pictures as they watched. About to ask for the score as he turned his attention back to the game, Hari stopped in amazement when he saw the umpire who was standing by the wicket on the bowler's side. The gray beret was distinctive.

"It's Morris!" Hari said. "How could I have missed him? He's an umpire."

"Indeed. I think he's enjoying it." Abdul added, "Morris used to think the game was too complicated, but now he knows all the rules. Kapil asked him to officiate. There are two umpires, of course."

Hari watched intently as the bowler—a medium pacer, it appeared—got ready to deliver the next ball in his over. Morris, wearing a full-sleeved white shirt, stood out of the bowler's way, and quietly faced the batsman. The batsman, his gaze somber as he took his position behind the crease line, clutched the bat with both hands and lightly tapped the pitch.

Before leaving Abdul's apartment the other day, Kapil had said, "Please remember that what we've been saying about Morris is between us."

"Of course," Hari had replied. "In any case, I'm not here to write about Morris."

Now those words came back to him. The bowler, having walked several yards as he rubbed the ball on his pants, stopped and turned to face the wickets. Morris, staying out of his path, was looking at the batsman. And the batsman was watching the bowler, expectantly. Running up to the stumps, the bowler spun his arm in a sweeping arc and released the ball. Just as the speeding ball hit the pitch and bounced, the batsman, moving gracefully, took a swing and tried to sweep it past the boundary for four runs.

But he missed completely—and the ball, flying past him, landed in the diving wicket-keeper's gloved hands. Rising swiftly, the wicket-keeper used his hands to dislodge the bails from the stumps on the batsman's side.

"HOWZAT!" the bowler cried, throwing his arms up as he jumped.

There was a roar from the stands, followed by a tense silence as everybody waited for the umpire's decision. Had the batsman been able to make it back safely by crossing the crease line before the bails got knocked off? Or did Kapil's team pick up another wicket? From his spot on the bench, Hari couldn't tell. Morris, however, knew the answer—and it wasn't a favorable one, as the groans in the vicinity indicated.

"Not out!" Morris said loudly and decisively, shaking his head.

# LAURA REDFORD

## *RETIRED*

When I tell people I am retired the next question is always,
"What did you do before?"

I never know what to say. I did none of those things that most people retire from.

I worked in garment factories, operating steam presses and fabric cutters. I worked in manufacturing plants, standing at moulding machines and sanders to produce a dozen different household items. I worked at wire mills, operating thirty-foot-long systems that produced cable as thick as my arm with the help of machinery twice as tall as I was.

I spent three years as an oiler on a tower crane, operated dirt compacters, scrapers, dozers and bobcats.

I drove a school bus, taught school as a substitute, worked in retail management, fast-food clean-up and waited tables. I worked at check-out registers at grocery stores and the check-in desk at a motel.

I worked for politicians, as administrative assistant to a lobbyist and then to a congresswoman.

I worked to live, and I lived. I lived and lived and lived some more.

I met all sorts of people, and many were my friends; white, black, Asian, and who-knows-what. We didn't care. I worked next to Jews, Catholics, fundamentalists, agnostics and who-knows-what. We didn't care.

I worked with a woman once who left early one day because her husband, making the kids a Chinese checkerboard with a power drill while seated, put a drill bit through his scrotum. I am sorry to say we found this hysterically funny. (His injury was minor.)

I worked with a woman who left early one day because her thirteen-year-old daughter had committed suicide.

I worked with a woman who kept me laughing all day long with her funny stories.

I worked with a woman who left work one day, walked out her back door and blew her face off with her husband's shotgun.

I worked with a WWII German war bride. I worked with an Auschwitz survivor. The war bride hated all Americans. The Auschwitz survivor could not take the strain of an assembly line and was returned to a mental facility.

I worked with black women and saw what it took to survive beneath that color.

And I learned. I learned and learned and learned.

I traveled to Europe, immersed in their cultures and loveliest of all, the London theater. I went to New York to experience Broadway.

In the end, I bought a farm. The idyll that had sustained me all the years before. In those years at the farm I was peed on, pooped on, spit and slobbered on, bit, scratched, knocked down and run over by every domestic critter known to man. And I prospered. I learned to invest in the stock market. And I prospered some more.

And now I write.

And I am retired.

The End (not quite)

# V
# PANDEMIC

# THE WAY WE LIVE NOW

# CLAUDE CLAYTON SMITH

## *A FRESHER CLIME*

> *... suppose*
> *Devouring pestilence hangs in our air*
> *And thou are flying to a fresher clime.*
> —Richard II, 1.3

I have come home for a while. The pandemic has closed the University. We have been returned to our parents, who don't want us either.

An email from Laura today. She sends her latest poem. Her images are brittle and delicate, yet they cut across the page like a Cossack's cry—pensive, tense, resplendent—all sensitivity and tact.

Laura is "stuck in Paris" due to Covid, on her junior year abroad. I am a great big senior, stuck at home. Where everything has stopped.

*Tu me manques*, she writes. I miss you, too.

The day is heavy and gray, legacy of this morning's storm. Summer-like thunder shook the first day of May after several days of sun. The lightning was unusually thin.

*M'aidez! M'aidez!* The climate is all out of whack.

This noon, while I was rereading Laura's email, a robin flew into the sun-porch screen with a chunky thud that startled me. Dazed, it glided to the fence, perched, hesitated, then dropped to the patio where, testing the flagstone, it recovered and hopped under the Adirondack chair to the forsythia bush. Later, having finished reading the letter, I noticed a noisy robin on the arched rose trellis.

A metaphor here perhaps: Life as interrupted flight.

The trellis needs a new coat of paint.

The pandemic has forced my father into early retirement, a less than golden handshake. The work he does is impossible from here. He slinks from room to room, avoiding me, strange mutual exiles that we are. Finely lined purple bubbles balloon from beneath his eyes. "The door is always open," he says, and does not question me.

My mother's world hasn't changed at all. It's just expanded by two. She calls Covid-19 the *Plandemic*, by which she means God's plan. "It's all in the Bible," she says. *"And great earthquakes shall be in divers places, and famines, and pestilences.* That's from Luke," she says, "21:11."

*Rich russet sun-ribbons twine*
*themselves around*
*dune oats and seaweed,*
*gray gulls and orange-creased crabs.*
*I walked on the watered edge*
*of the sand and noticed the sunlight*
*falling away to each side . . .*

From Laura's poem. I will reply with the suggestion to drop the *ed* on *walked* and *noticed* because there is no *ed* on *twine*.

Subtle image of the sunlight parting.

The cloudiness continues. In the back yard I notice a broken branch near the top of the maple tree, snapped by the storm. I take a ladder, a saw, and ascend. The leaves are wet. I jar the limbs and they shower me, as if in spite for intruding. I grip the trunk with one hand and saw away with the other. The shower mixes with sawdust and blinds me.

Later, the tree looks raped.

"Your father will appreciate that," my mother says. "He can't climb because of his back. All that surgery for a herniated disc. The tree will mend.

Your father mended."

What is the point here?

Mother-voice announces water in the basement. I mop for an hour. My father argues the need for repairs. The argument is trivial and ends with everybody shouting.

I finish mopping and excuse myself. Go upstairs to the sun porch to read from Isaac Babel. *Red Calvary*. Those incredible Cossacks.

Sudden darkness and driving rain again. From the sun porch I solve the problem of water in the basement. The corner drainpipe is overflowing, spilling water all along the eaves. The drain is clogged. A small lake has formed at the base of the cellar window, hence the mess downstairs.

I put on a hooded yellow slicker, take the ladder from the garage, a length of BX cable from the cellar, and ascend. The rain beats hard on my head. My parents watch from the sun porch. I shove the BX cable down the drainpipe and flush out a bird's nest.

My parents stare at me, puzzled. I point at the ground and shout through the rain: *"It was only a bird's nest!"* But the rain comes down hard and they cannot hear me.

Laura asks if I miss making love. She writes of our last time together, before she left for France. That long afternoon out in the country. Pre-pestilence. Not knowing when we'd make love again. The idea of *when* has been extended indefinitely.

I once asked Laura what it was like for her when we made love. She said, *It's every color, every noise, every pain, every thrill. It feels like I'm going in all directions all at once and can't get out of my skin fast enough.*

I told her she should write that down.

From Laura's earlier work:

*Sun-slapped flower faces*
*quickly sunburn.*
*Fraying softly, rust-singed laces*
*fold precisely in their places,*
*topple to earth as cotton maces—*
*wind-blown clouds in great sky-spaces . . .*

Laura sees everything as a child does: For the first time.

Sunday morning is sunny and clear. My father drives my mother to church. Reads the paper in the car while she attends to business inside.

I decide there is a need for a dry well at the base of the drainpipe by the corner of the house. I dig a hole three feet deep, take an old garbage can, chisel out the bottom, and sink the cylinder in the hole. The soil is mostly gravel. There is little dirt left once I have screened the debris. I fill the cylinder with stones and level it off.

A neighbor wanders over from next door, masked like an hombre in a Western. He keeps six feet away. Wants to know what all the bangings about. I tell him I was chiseling out the bottom of a garbage can. Hold up the jagged disc.

"Be here long?" he says.

"As long as it takes."

"It's good to have you around," he says, but I can tell he's not so sure.

## LAURA APOL

### *ODE TO THE HERON*

> *If we . . . for once could do nothing,*
> *perhaps a huge silence*
> *might interrupt this sadness*
> *of never understanding ourselves*
> —Pablo Neruda, "Keeping Quiet"

Someone should tell the trees
we are sheltered in place. Each day
they nudge further
toward green, toward tenuous blossom
in the reckless spring wind.

Someone should tell the heron, and the light
on the heron;

someone should tell the wild hyacinths,
the beaded grace of the willow: *this is the year*
*for unfettered beauty. Do not hold back.*

Consider the lilies. Consider the robin,
the redbud and magnolia. Consider
the vole and the feral cat and the fox
poised at the verge.

Praise the immovable
rock in the river, the bones
of the fallen fir. Bless the iridescent blue
beetle. Step gently.

And study the heron—            she flies
where she will    head forward, full-on

wings herself in reverse
to slow,           stop
then settle
              serene and unblinking
in the fast-moving current.

## SIX SUITES FOR UNACCOMPANIED CELLO

The young mother peels
potatoes in the playroom, surrounded
by her four boys. Their stories
compete as she fingers the kennebecs

in the bowl. She takes in all
their voices at once, yet listens to each—
postpones silence until there is silence
to be found. Her own thoughts surface then,

and she'll know what she knows
about love—to keep a part for herself:
a few fumbling notes
on the cello she is just beginning to learn,

a lesson she embraces one hour
each week. She does not choose scales
or the rasp of simple tunes, selects instead
Bach's solo suites, their ravenous

scope and sweep. She guides the bow
with fierce attention, crosses strings
with singular care. Just one note,
then another—

the press of each measure ongoing,
insatiable.

# KRISTY SNEDDEN

## *BABBLE*

Nesting dolls are everywhere,
a set in my office, deep rose,
another at home.

In my car they spill emerald
across the seat onto the floor,
roll to the back.

I look for a suitcase. There are
dolls asleep in each of them,
bright orange and red.

I locked these hollow dolls with
smokey blue to keep the secrets.
Is there a better justification?

All my life I saved them
with warm indigo washes,
even the shadows.

When the dolls shake,
I build an earthquake
of fire opal just for them.

They call to me
at awkward times.
Persistent dolls.

Let me out.
Let me be.
Let me.

## RAVEN CLIFFS

The third time I hiked to the cliffs

the light pulled me to that place

that lives on the edge of time.

Ahead on the trail was a man

whose cat wrapped around his neck

and it was impossible to tell

where the cat ended and the man's neck

began. I was hiking with my friend

whose dark hair falls to her hips

and shades of green and gold wove in

and out, tiny snakes making their

nests. As we approached the top

of the cliffs, a small cave caught my eye.

We sat there to eat our tangerines.

The juice was my mouth and my

tongue was the fruit. At the very top

I saw a fledgling Eastern Bluebird

who flew into my chest. Now I

chirp during the week and hop

from branch to branch. Sometimes

my skin glints blue in the light.

## LAURA SHOVAN

*PANDEMIC MORNING*

A falling dream. Eyes open,
I breathe. Into my waking space
you growl, still asleep.
I throw one hand toward you.
My fingers make contact
with your nose, forehead,
closed eyes. "Nightmare?"
I ask as you flinch awake.
"Someone was at the door." We talk
without looking at each other,
turn on the lights, begin our day.

## WALKING BACK FROM THE MAILBOX

I shelter beneath the magnolia tree,
hold my body quiet in the shadow
of its wide leaves. Wood smoke
spills from neighbors' houses.
Winter stings my nose, settles
in my lungs. I stand here
because ice is falling fast.
Percussive beads strike
the wide, waxy leaves.
The sound is new to me and so
I stand beneath the magnolia tree
and, for a moment, cease to be.

## WAITING ROOM

TVs mounted on the walls.
A morning news show.
The host laughs.

It's still beating, the heart.
A heart is not enough
to make one viable

outside the body.
This is what the doctor said.
For a while, the future

was where I spooled
my thoughts—let
threads tumble forward

in time until they
formed themselves
into finished garments,

sewn up hems. The jacket
my son might wear,
my daughter's summer dress—

the one who is not viable.
There is only this room. The television.
Nurses busy at the desk.

The morning show shifts
to the ten day forecast,
a late snow moving in.

## ZOE SINGER

### *INTERMISSION*

When the curtain fell down
in our bedroom
I left it.

Icy air and a pandemic
without and across
from us: windows.

In lit boxes other people's
houseplants and
those moments when

they drop their pants
or work out with
a video

or fight with large
arm movements like
stilted puppets.

I wake in the night
to see someone hunched
over his screen

like a man in a Western
cupping a flame
to a cigarette in the wind.

Huddled searching
that blurs time,
dries the mouth
and eyes,
promises the world.

All of our longing,
backlit.

## AND WE

*Greenwood Cemetery, March 2021*

Hawks circling in a whipping wind
above trees over graves and we
wandering between the things we
see and cannot reach

They tack wingtips and fanned tail in
a tightening coil overhead
teasing the top leaves barely
formed by early spring

and, as sometimes happens, we begin
to scent the crematorium—
a sweet wrong smoke meeting the yeast
of the bakery across the street

It is late March and
we want and we
want and we
want.

## LOIS BAER BARR

*THURSDAY MORNING REFLECTION*

I decided to write at my dressing table
                                   the idea tickled me so
I could barely sleep          thought of the time
I was three and sleepwalked to my parents' room
peed on the white ruffled stool at Mommy's vanity

thought of the mahogany vanity with a big oval mirror
                                   in Bubby's apartment
her box of Coty powder, Ponds Cold Cream, rouge
                                   an ivory hand mirror
I think the handle was cracked    I think it wasn't
ivory                          I must get to sleep so I can
get up and write before I fix our breakfast
                                   oops, it's 8 a.m., too late

"Where are you writing today?"
"At my dressing table . . ."
"What?" Lew almost spits out his coffee,
"If I live to be a hundred, I still won't get you."

                                   I shrug
he gets me, he gets me, but he wants me to
                                   think bigger
                                   work bigger
                                   wear brighter colors
                                   put on lipstick

the stool at my cramped dressing table has a
slatted view of our quiet street through mini blinds
the rain has stopped since I walked our puppy

I wrote a haiku as we walked and committed it
to memory reciting aloud                she liked it

> *red maple leaves join yellow*
>     *as the rain*
> *paints a street mural*

                              oops, only fourteen syllables

it feels funny to sit here        I never take time getting ready
I apply sunscreen, some blush, and run
                        lipstick goes on in the car

lovely view              I should work here more often

here's Mom's Estee Lauder Private Collection Parfum
an acorn given to everyone in Dorianne Laux's
workshop at Kentucky Women Writers
a three-inch Statue of Liberty
                        souvenir of cycling
                        from home to NYC
about ten years ago Lew announced we would
take that ride on his seventieth birthday
*he'll forget*               I thought
                     he didn't

                     Lew works big
he makes veggie soup in a twelve-quart pot
he makes biscotti for friends and packs them
                     in silver tins
                     he delivers

as I write this, Lew's vacuuming the house
he's coming closer        the dog proceeds him
Lew grabs my Happy Camper flipflop to mock me,
"Oh, the stories this flipflop could tell!"
puppy would like to grab the other flipflop
                        she knows better

                              I tune them out
                              keep writing

tucked behind the Kleenex box there's a map
                              Elk County Trails
that's from Ridgway, PA where Lew learned to carve
                              with a chainsaw
he carved a bear cub coming out of a tree stump
I walked on the trails with the chainsaw master's wife
a gray day like today          trillium had pushed up
Liz Boni knew the birds' nests, the old sawmill

    *getting wet on river trail*
        *two gray heads*
 *poems surround us*

we sat in her Jeep listening to her poetry
set to music by a friend in Nashville

    *I'm grateful for the sun and soil   D*
    *The rain that makes love grow   C#m*
    *And I will always share with you   D/E*
    *The garden of my soul   A\**

first time I sat in a car with anyone
other than family since Covid19 began
we'd known each other a few hours, but I
connected to her heart as I heard her songs
busy talking, Liz ran two stop signs, missed a turn

on my windowsill, tiny paintings Mom and Dad bought
from an old neighbor        one is a Vanitas
                              without the skull
I prefer this one                 like a Dutch still life
golden apples in a copper bowl on a dark table
he must have used a size 0 sable brush

I don't work in oils, just watercolors
                         I work small
                         write flash fiction
                         essayettes

but for Lew's birthday I painted the Alhambra
on a big leftover square of plywood
sanded, gessoed, painted one side with acrylics,
didn't like it, prepped, and painted the other
       MOUNTAINS PURPLE WALLS YELLOW
             SKY BLUE
       PERSPECTIVE SKEWED

the first week of quarantine, Lew thought we should
                         paint a mural
we stood in line at ACE terrified of everyone
got rollers, brushes, masking tape, quart of white, pints of color:
                         sun kissed yellow
                         turquoise haze
                         lipstick red
                         black knight
taped and prepped the wall on ladders
painted the Sierra Nevada a lavender hue
                         with snowy peaks
in the foreground a field of
                         big red poppies
a hit on Facebook           *perspective off kilter*
*like my tussles with POV*    I thought
oh well, painting is my pleasure
                         poetry's my table
a vanity where I sit and look in the mirror

---

*\*I am grateful to Liz Boni for allowing me to quote her song which was adapted and set to music by Rob Simbeck. Her poetry is in We Should Go There (2021) by Liz Boni and Josie Feikls.*

# SHARON D. SHELTZER

### *LIFE IN A DUMPSTER*

Moving. Just say the word and it brings up visceral reactions in almost everyone. Shivers and eyerolls. Why is it that when you spend the weekend away with a small bag loosely packed with a change or two of clothes, a toothbrush, lipstick, book, and purse with cell phone, you have everything needed for your stay? Well, maybe a bicycle secured to the car back too. And in my case, I've been living in our future retirement home almost halftime for six years, sparsely furnished but complete for comfortable living, reveling in the glorious spareness, yet when it comes time to make the final move, there are boxes and bags of items that somehow become essential. Husband says, "Moving is very hard for me, I need to take my time and go through everything. I don't want a time limit—we'll be done when we're done." I say, "We should just give everything away and it will be easier."

He doesn't start until a few weeks after his retirement, spending some time in our newish home on the Bay, and then vacationing in Hawaii. I would like to get on with it, having been waiting for five years, but hey, we've been married for thirty-nine years, and I know when to bend. I promise myself that I won't tear my hair out while tearing apart the house. It takes about three months of concentrated effort once we begin, and it is unlike anything I have ever experienced.

Twenty years of living in our 1937 saltbox style house on Main Street in the smallish city of Visalia, in the Central Valley of California. Seventeen years before that in the quaint town of Three Rivers, thirty minutes up the hill from Visalia, living in a self-designed house while raising our two boys. A total of thirty-seven years of accumulated life and memories. We saved almost everything from our first country house and deposited it into the voluminous storage space in our city home. The clutter increased through the years thanks to free delivery by Amazon. We will need to fit everything into our half-sized, already furnished house in our funky but beautiful bay-town.

Moving phases:

1. Don't need to bring anything. I say—"What I love about our new house is that it is uncluttered."

2. I begin to crack—"However, I admit, we could use a few extra kitchen utensils."

3. Inability to separate objects from memories—Even I come around to understanding that our memories define our lives—"Maybe you were right we need a storage unit."

"Nevertheless, my mantra still is, "If you can't imagine where it will go in our new house, then give it away."

We have a front yard sale for two days. It is amazing what people will buy. A small rock engraved with the word Harmony. Old shoes. Watercolors I dashed off years ago. Outdated technology. Since we live on Main Street, there is a lot of traffic. Husband seems remarkably calm about parting with this first pass of stuff, which is mostly useless to us. We practically give things away but still make $2,000. The next week we spend preparing for our estate sale to clear out a house full of furniture and valuable items. Our estate sale manager is an old acquaintance who, it turns out, no longer lives up to her excellent reputation. Age affects us all. Many items are left untagged, especially the harder to reach ones upstairs, and she overprices the others. My family does all the arranging, cleaning, and sign placement, and disassembles and carries the furniture down the stairs. I buy the lunches and take in the money, tracking every item. She schmoozes, smokes cigarettes, tells us what to do, sits on the stairs to rest and keeps her 45%, relying on my son and daughter-in-law to do all the heavy lifting. Both my boys and their new wives help, and we have a ball amidst the chaos. Our family teeters between having a lot of laughs at her expense and being mildly annoyed. One daughter-in-law was more than a little piqued, starting a fight with her on my behalf. Although I could stand up for my opinion about slashing furniture prices, it was sweet that she defended me. Luckily for him (and us), Husband is out of town this weekend. He would have balked at people rummaging through our house. I am glad every time someone walks out with their arms full; less for us to deal with. We even find a buyer for the house during the estate sale. Even though much remained unsold, selling the house was more than worth the effort.

Meanwhile, the rented trash bin is filled and emptied three times over the last intense month that includes the two sale events. The whole family found it was best to do this when Husband was gone, although occasionally he proudly notifies us when he adds something to the bin. I text photos of items to friends who are opening Airbnb's. I'm beginning to realize that I do care about my stuff—I want my friends to have things that are special to me. I tell a stranger during the estate sale that they made a wise choice— the artist in the drawing they just bought is renowned in Mexico for his political commentary. I remember meeting him and how he bestowed me with this sketch, which I carefully brought back from my Spanish-learning trip to Mexico. I tell another buyer about the Berlin wall memento from our German exchange student. I smile when my daughters-in-law request to keep a special mirror or basket. "Are you sure you don't want the china too?" It took us months to find the right dining room table to fit in our high ceilinged, square room with pickled window casings. I care about that process so much that I refuse to sell it during the estate sale, wanting to offer the beautiful table to the family who will buy our house. And of course, there is the black and white polka dot rug in the bedroom with matching wallpaper. Joy, the house buyers want the rug, but disappointment, not the table. More posting on Marketplace and Craigslist. I am tied to my phone, answering inane questions about the size of a desk that was clearly posted as 2'x3'.

My goal was to limit the stuff we moved to our coastal house to one or two car trips, each time integrating it into our half-empty shelves, bookcases, and file cabinets. So far, I've made four trips with my SUV stuffed to the gills, requiring the rear-view mirror to be shifted to the camera mode. Receipts from donations all over town are spilling out of my purse. Order of events is fill up my car with donated items and deliver before we pack the car with things we will try to shoehorn into our formerly uncluttered cabinets.

Of course, the photos and albums must come. What about other mementos? These include plaques, items from multiple trips abroad, gifts from exchange students, everything related to the kids, lots of letters, grade school through college remembrances, old projects, and files. Then there are entire categories of stuff.

Books: There is a lot of discussion about our expansive library, some books so old their covers have disintegrated. Husband says, "I have to cull through each one to make a decision which to bring." I will be dead before he finishes. Husband continues, "We don't have enough bookshelves in our new house (which is half the size of our Valley home); design flaw!" He smiles. I get to work on designing new shelves that we can squeeze into our modestly sized bedroom. He also says, "I can get rid of the doubles." Sub-text: nothing else. Relenting a little, he delivers boxes of books to the Woman's Auxiliary, but even I feel the need to hang on to the remainder.

Sports equipment: This includes backpacking gear, car camping items, skis, poles, boots, windsurfer, helmets, racer bars, locks, pumps. Some of these will join our bicycles, sailing and kayak accessories already in our Bay-town shed. Son #2 suggests that we saw the old windsurfer into half and put it in our rented dumpster. I am OK with that, but Husband grimaces like his arm is being dismembered. Lots of memories sailing in San Francisco Bay, boarding from Alameda Harbor to Angel Island. I remember the time my windsurfer drifted under the Golden Gate Bridge when the powerful breezes prevented me from lifting the sail out of the water. Kind rescuers tipped their Hobie Cat while trying to save me, and ironically, I helped them right their boat, being a more proficient sailor than board rider. Son cuts trusty old board into four parts with his portable saw while we are gone driving my car full of stuff to the bay-town. He sends a photo of the chopped windsurfer topping off the full dumpster. Husband gasps. Next, what to do with the perfectly good windsurf sails? At the moment, they are still in our Valley garage—one more week to make a decision.

Tools: Old ones are donated to Habitat for Humanity or Goodwill, but several must be packed. Especially the chop saw that I received from Husband for Mother's Day. I know there is no room for the stand. How did we accumulate so many screws and nails and extension cords? We must save the battery charger. That will come in handy one day. Thankfully Son #2 guides Husband through the task of disassembling the garage contents. It would be impossible for me to motivate him to accomplish that chore. In addition to tools, he has boxes of work material, certificates, diplomas, and framed photographs that he removed from his offices. The highlight of this effort was when a homeless guy passed by our open garage door and asked if he could have our tent that we were setting up on the sidewalk.

Files and drawings: I throw away my work files after extracting a few especially nice drawings and sketches. I do save documents cataloging our recent bay-town house construction. The process of eliminating thirty-five years of architecture drawings takes months; first advertising in my hometown newspaper for my clients to collect their original house plans and then delivering some of them. I look through the rolled drawings, admiring the fine drafting and notice that my skills peaked in my forties before my fingers started to go numb. I decided to keep a set that was particularly beautiful, and the two sets that were our own houses. Then I toss the rest into the recycle bin. Husband says that when I am famous after my death, I will be sorry. He puts off scouring his voluminous files. We have a large office/cottage that served as my office for many years, with drawers and drawers of file space, mostly occupied by his stuff—I preferred to keep my files on the counters to keep them separate. Then thankfully he decides to scan his life's research and history. This takes a week, but it does solve one space problem. He disappears into the office each day; twenty thousand pages scanned. This effort was different than most moving tasks, so he was almost happy. Will he finish before the house cleaners come?

Letters: I am reminded of how we used to write letters instead of sending emails and texts. And all of them are in cursive writing. Bags of correspondence from lifelong friends, but what about the six-page letters from a girl I can't remember until prompted by Husband, and the letter from the younger brother of a former neighbor, pouring out his heart to me about his attempted suicide? I don't remember him either. I puzzle over that. I am embarrassed by a letter I wrote in my twenties but reassured that I was smart enough not to send it. I reluctantly throw that one out, not wanting my kids to see it, but save the rest. I am breaking my own rule—I have no idea where these will go.

As I sift through my work files, I remember projects and clients. Did I fulfill my potential as an architect? Was it the right choice to put family before work? Family photos reassure my choices. I can't throw those away. Did Husband love me as much as I think? Card after saved card reassures me. Did I give enough to my community? Plaques, taken off my office walls, provide testament to this. My adult sons go through their saved schoolwork and drawings. They are delighted. We read letters I wrote to their principal and teachers. We reminisce about old friends, and it is bonding for us all to remember those times. Especially fun are the photos of Son #1 in his preschool class picture, with his then three-year-old future wife two seats away. I am asked, "How terrible is the moving process?" I pause, realizing there has been a shift, "It's less about moving and more about remembering, not really so bad. A time for reflection between one part of life and another." Maybe Husband's admonition to take it easy, wasn't off the mark.

## GAYLORD BREWER

### *IN TIME OF CRISIS AND QUARANTINE, THE INSISTENCE OF SMALL THINGS*

 I get lucky, steal two hours between storms to mow a section of the ragged spring lawn, a rebuking mess with weed, wild onion, and shaggy clump. I've even spare minutes to get fussy, trim along the foundation and the garden's wooly edge. A little disorder temporarily put right. What I can contribute before the rains, which seem they will never stop, rains that have moved far beyond metaphor for our helpless gloom to merely embellish the world's dark and tallied announcements, return to banish me to our home transformed to comfortable prison. My wife, meanwhile, attacks her writing room with a fastidious fury. Organizing files, straightening books, polishing shelves and frames, dust rag and vacuum. She soaks the globes of the miniature oil lamps in soapy water. Wipes clean the boots of the Russian doll in mink cap I brought her from St. Petersburg, from a different life. Small things to stave off the hand that trembles on its own, then stops. The blade of argument flashed over nothing. The sudden intake of breath, a panicked heart. It's a jumble. A mess of fragments. Forgive me. The pressed button on the radio and the news topping each unforeseeable hour. The bruising isolation of intimacy, of disembodiment. On and on. Nothing remains to ironize. Satire has a sour taste. To pause. To exhale. Unclench that hand. To strive to be patient and kind. Before the sky closes in again, I look across the manicured square of green, its neat edges. It is glowing. Further, our scraggly forsythias have never looked so effusive, so beautiful, have never, I believe, tried so hard. I cheer them on in gratitude. Yellow has no desire for subtlety. Yellow just wants to be happy. Fragments. Shadows. Fear. When, sweaty and aching from my work, I reenter the house, I smell the pungent lemon polish, see the dusting cloth crumbled on the carpet like—again, forgive me—vanquished flag or soiled shroud of the dead. What I mean to say is, the polish smells clean and good. Insistent. A drum of thunder in the sky. However many hours remaining before today is done.

## MANOIR SUR-LE-CAP

Sipping a smooth but woodsy Québécois gin, a plate of smoked salmon and sturgeon and a good mystery on the side table, warm in soft flannel I sit still in the rocking chair before the fire. Downstairs—it's a three-story suite, four if you count the mudroom for boots and coats—my wife soaks in the whirlpool tub. An afternoon of walking in the cold and snow of the Plains of Abraham, of shopping for gifts, of hot mulled wine balanced in stiff hands at the German Christmas Market. In an hour, a reservation at a favorite, intimate restaurant, a taxi to guide us there, coin for every cost and generous tips. What more to say, really, regarding this life of absurd privilege? I am practiced in excess, good at sensual pleasure, but also at the dark mood, the rent moment, the blade artfully delivered. I taste the botanicals on my tongue, watch the fire writhe and gasp.

Then, as is my habit these past five years of holiday, I walk to the double doors of the balcony, open them toward me, and step into the pleasant sting of early night. I gaze past the blue-lit spruce perennially on display, over a white rooftop and across the St. Lawrence, a river I fear and love. On the opposite shore, atop the hill, the scattered lights of Lévis, better from a distance. The ferries keep the river from freezing, break passage through shelves of ice. A boat crosses now, slow, deliberate, its reflection small on the black water. The river's majestic indifference and beatitude of danger.

## *DARKNESS*

This winter condition, for lack of better phrase, remains on me. Perhaps not a darkness so much as a silence, a restive animal, an uninflected distance. I've no excuse, no right to it. Bright January afternoon. The world sunshine and roses. And yet. Walking the countryside makes no difference, the great texts, the austerity of the fast, the amateur's attempt at mindfulness. Certainly no discussion of a trite and popular rebirth. And not seasonal, either. The last time the fist seized me was on an island in Brazil. July. Heaven. And not a thing I would call depression, and certainly not despair, but a sort of . . . what? Wariness? An unspecified foreboding? And neither does it lack an ironic perspective, moments of humor and recognition. Whether the cause be chemical, mental, spiritual, or other is of no interest to me. I have learned to remain quiet—in breathing, in thought, in movement. To listen and wait. Trust the gestures. Better, too, all possible distance from the human comedy. As necessary: smile, nod, move away, reveal nothing. Keep hands open and still. When it arrives at home, though, I feel bad for Lucy, so keenly attuned to my mood. I stroke her fur and ask patience. Assure her all will be well.

## TOMORROW WOULD BE A LONG DAY

Fiddling at the stove with my bachelor dinner, believing you'd already left, I was surprised by the single honk that brought me and dog Lucy to the door. We watched you pull away. And suddenly, choke of dust rising from beneath tires, my favorite cover of the Dylan song harmonious in the room, my throat contracted. I couldn't swallow, my breath was short, and I was overcome. The parched gravel drive, the car receding, receding, turning from view. You were gone. And although I knew the scene I watched was fantasy, I saw it no less vividly: You leaving us, hatchback askew with boxes and books, lamps and pillows, tears and anger at lives never to be put back together, the stupid waste of it all. And I stood there, blinking, foolish, staring at the empty passage. How grateful was I that, instead, you were merely off to the city for the evening, a play in rehearsal, my dinner a one-off mess rather than a long horizon of lonely meals. I checked the burners, began the song again, and returned to bolt the door. Two young does ambled into the drive, sampling perimeter plants. We rarely see deer here anymore, but there they were— lovely, alive, curious, chastising my indulgence. In a few hours you'd be home. No separation, no collision. I'd probably be asleep, a little drunk. But outdoor lights to welcome you, the hot and sour soup you love in the fridge. Into your pajamas, hello, a bit of TV to unwind. And in the future, however distracted you are with thoughts of your script, the director, the inexperienced actors, my harshness, our rituals of disregard, you can kiss me good-bye twice any time you like. What a long day tomorrow would be, indeed, what a crooked trail, if otherwise.

## LOU STOREY

### *INVITING SANCTUARY*

"This is my sanctuary," my four o'clock client said. I felt much the same and said so. When I first started my private practice as a psychotherapist, I knew I wanted more than just a desk, a chair, a couch, and a long wooden bench in the waiting room. Working with a local realtor, my answer to what I was looking for in square footage was somewhat cryptic, "An area that can contain a good measure of calm, quiet, and an allowance for stillness."

And I found it. Three bright windowed rooms overlooking a marine park. Views of sky and river. I filled these rooms with rich earth tones of ochre and mahogany, choosing fabrics generous in tactile delight, blanketing the floors in late autumn colors and deep forest moss. I wanted my office to be like a symphony hall, designed to amplify the practiced efforts of string, wind, and percussion while keeping clean and pure the importance of the hushed moments, the silences linking notes that binds it all together.

My first career was in the arts. Art school in New York City had been a thrilling adventure of exploration and experimentation in the material world of creation: palettes of rich pigmented paint and feathery sable brushes, spinning wheels of slippery clay, indelible inks, the pull of silkscreens, learning the weaves of fine linen and coarse canvas. The goal of self-expression required a similar level of exploration, a soul search that questioned, if art is communication, what do I genuinely want to say? Followed by the more difficult question: is what I am creating conveying what I intend?

"Go to a museum and look at people looking at art," our Introduction to Painting professor instructed the class. Noting our confusion, she added, "if you pay close attention, I promise you will learn something vital."

I have no idea who actually did or did not do this assignment. I did. Coming from a family thin on religious affiliation, museums for me filled the void of a need for sublime communion and spiritual replenishment. Entering the Metropolitan Museum, I chose five galleries and spent an hour of subtle people-watching in each. Like a sociologist looking to decipher the link connecting humans and art, I took a seat and watched. My painting professor's promise held true. As the uniformed museum guard made her way, room to room, giving the ten minutes to closing warning, I was pleased to be leaving, having learned something new and strange.

I did my best the following week to articulate to the class what I had witnessed. "You see someone suddenly stop, turn toward a work of art as if the piece had just tapped them on the shoulder. Face to face with the artwork, their posture shifts, jaw loosens, and lips part. The air joining viewer and art becomes charged as if both painting and person break free from the limit of physical state to meet and mingle somewhere in that fertile gap. I could sense in the viewer an urgency to hold that opening, enlarge the moment, resist the inevitable return to the here and now."

Except for the professor and a few of the nicer students, I recall my effort at explanation being met with a good degree of teasing and gentle mockery. My frustration was not so much about their response but with my own inability to explain a phenomenon for which I had no adequate vocabulary. The experience left me with a sense of wonder toward the mystery of what can be felt but not seen.

My day in the museum had other benefits as well. Observing a woman around my age removing one of the paintings and then posting a "Temporarily Removed" sign, I ventured to ask, how does someone end up working in a museum? "Well, if you are an art student," she said, sizing me up correctly, "just ask at the front desk for an application to be an art handler." I was in awe. A handler of art! Like a jeweler awash in precious stones or a wrangler and her horses, I could think of no better job than becoming a citizen in the community of art. I joined up.

Part-time museum work opened into full-time employment after graduation. Art handler was just one of many positions needed to run a museum. Before working in a museum, I had only shared the space with other visitors and the art. I never suspected the intricate hierarchy of talented people whose hard work was, by intention, seen only in the results. I soon wanted more than handling the art. The creative urge that prompted me to paint and exhibit my art did not stop at the door of my studio. I wanted to do the same in the museum, be a designer of exhibitions.

For twenty-five years in various towns, cities, and states, I collaborated with museums, libraries, schools, and institutions. Each looked to house exhibitions that could communicate something of relevance to their public. Exhibitions can be many things. Historical, philosophical, biographical, didactic, issue-related, or purely a display of art. Each exhibition required that I listen and pay close attention to what wanted to be said. The core of my work involved finding and intensifying what I saw as the relationship that unites the viewer with the art, constructing a bridge between stimulus and response. The end goal for the public was not so much education as it was to bring together the ingredients that could foster inspiration.

And then I retired, but not to the pleasures of Bingo or a rocking chair. I returned to school to earn a master's in social work and a doctorate in psychology. What looked to others like a bold leap was for me an obvious next step. Nearly three decades of listening, observing, bringing two things together to form that miracle where "the whole is greater than the sum of its parts" felt like good preparation for the role of psychotherapist.

Just as in art school, I was again given a valuable suggestion from a wise professor in my Human Behavior class. "Sometimes we have so much to say to the client, we can fill the air with our own brilliance," she explained, "but is that what we are there for? When you feel that urge, try imagining four bold letters right above your client's head. W. A. I. T." The professor then smiled and unpacked the acronym. "Why Am I Talking?"—an excellent question to keep in the forefront of my practice. I needed to develop an allowance for stillness, to sit in peaceful acceptance of those verbal pauses that bring about a deepening, the way a tea bag needs time to steep to reach full flavor. With great care, I had put together a physical location, something more than an office, that could comfortably honor those instances where words drop away, allowing silence to communicate.

None of us could have anticipated the effects of a virus so lethal it could spread with the rapidity of mold engulfing an orange, a global tragedy that shut down the world. The words "resilience," "endurance," and "patience" circulated person to person in a thousand different languages. We adjusted, reframing loss as change, yet death tendered no soothing conversion.

My office was no longer able to offer sanctuary. Those who could fit our worlds into the offerings of modern technology reduced our polychromatic public lives down to a monochrome of home and the flat rectangle of screen.

"I lost my sanctuary," my client lamented over Zoom. Can it be found again in some new way? Is "calm" a reasonable expectation for someone in an apartment too small to give equally what is needed to each family member?

Is "serenity" a fair request from someone whose job, now furloughed, may never return? Is "stability" even possible in the reality of family members lost to sudden death, hospitals and schools unable to fulfill core missions, world events taking a jackhammer to peace of mind?

"Better than nothing," we said. The one-second delay of computer audio, the erratic moments of visual freeze, the annoying static of digital interruptions—I could no longer anticipate that usual pause inherent in dialogue, was unable to continue the practice of W.A.I.T. to nurture what grows in silence. What had been natural needed to become intentional. "Let's give ourselves a long moment, eyes closed. Give allowance to the sounds, the distractions, the interruptions, knowing they can, in some personal way, be included in your sanctuary." A noble effort, but with intention comes expenditure of energy, leaving most of us in some degree of exhaustion. We find ways to recharge.

My dog and I are both old by any ordinary standard, but we don't dwell on it. Sitting together on a small porch overlooking the street, my dog lifts his silky head skyward. Nostrils flair, capturing a squirrel in the maple tree, car exhaust and roadkill, brick dust, pigeon feathers, and the damp possibility of rainclouds.

I too lean my head back, sharing his experience, open to the unknowing of time as a clockface, willing to allow one simple moment to be the measure of a life.

## MICHAEL HETTICH

*A SHARPER SHADOW*

Sometimes when we sit without talking for a while
the light seems to fall through the trees with a different
sense of itself. What I mean is, I feel
something of the *tenuous,* even in our silence,
as though we were counting our breaths, preparing
ourselves to let go of each other, maybe

sooner than we know. This ache feels more deeply
interfused than love, though of course it is love too.
I think what I mean is, it casts a sharper shadow
than love, even love that lasts a lifetime. Maybe
it's like a map of being, deeply-etched wood-grain,

or the way snow falls into a field of uncut grasses
through the stillness of an afternoon: Something in that light
moves into the shape of things and changes their contours
as dusk rises to meet the sky—
and the snow falls all night, to glow in the morning,
trackless but shadowed by the gently-blowing grass.

## CERTAIN HARMONIES

When I walk through our town these evenings, I imagine
I can listen to my neighbors chattering inside
their houses, recounting their days while they cook
dinner, sip a cocktail, or watch TV.
I've lived alone now for so many years
I hardly talk to anyone, unless I'm explaining
my troubles to the squirrels and the trees—and since
I have few troubles, I mostly walk in silence.

Sometimes I venture out beyond our town,
where the stars shine brighter and the animals are wild.

I stand still and try to remember who I was,
but mostly I just listen to the music in my head,
old love songs from the days when I felt like cliché
could rise to revelation, a quiver in the voice
at just the right moment
was a baring of the soul.

Sometimes certain harmonies can seem to shape the world,
I think, as a heron squawks up and flies off,
darker than the darkness it disappears into.
I still myself and try to hear the beating of its heart,
the rush of the night through its wings. By the time
I turn to walk home, most houses are silent

so I listen to the moths beat themselves against the streetlights,
the songbirds breathe in the trees.

## *PALIMPSEST*

A sapling in a copse of larger trees
at the edge of a mid-winter, snow-dusted field
holds its withered, desiccated leaves
to the thin light and the wind, though those leaves
are skeletons, x-rays of lost hands, their translucent
flesh tattered and fallen away:

the light of stained glass on a cold Sunday morning,
an ancient parchment we squint to read,
whose language we can't know. The tree won't let go—
as though its leaves might never die
if they could be held until spring.  And how many

days in your own life will quicken and wake you?
How many days will you hold up what you've loved
in yourself and lost while you loved it? Maybe

that's why we walk out on half-frozen lakes
when dusk holds still, before giving way to darkness.
That's how we learn to be lighter than air
for just a moment—to make it to the other side.

## THE RIVER

I'm taking a pause from the person I've been
for most of my life, and starting to enter
the man I've been only occasionally, even
the man I've only pretended to be—
a stranger I've hardly imagined.

My wife has decided to do the same.
We've agreed to try out our new selves, and meet
back here in a few days, to talk things over,
perhaps make some permanent adjustments.

Our children might be strangers soon.
Our old dog already ignores us.

The river that runs by our house has been rising
for weeks now. We've been cleaning out our closets,
tossing things into the swirl:
old books we thought we should love, classics
that only bored us, as they've bored everyone
for centuries. Photo albums full of squinting strangers,
dress shoes that pinched, overstuffed pillows
that made our necks stiff. And then, one morning,

a herd of deer tried to swim across to our side.
So many hungry animals have been swept away.

Even our faces in the mirror seem
to have been swept away now, by that rising river
and by our yearning. I can only be naked,
though I'm trying to locate the clothes I wore
when I was a man who sported perfect teeth
and a full head of hair, the kind who tells the truth
when he lies—or vice-versa, I can't remember now,
though I'm sure it must matter to someone.

## A MOMENT IN HISTORY

# MK PUNKY

## *PANDEMIC (TRUST)*

When the pandemic paralyzed our world
we all enjoyed an abundance of newly reclaimed time
to evaluate the importance and necessity of our daily toils

When the pandemic paralyzed our world
we all witnessed our richest and most powerful leaders
stripped naked of pretensions

When the pandemic paralyzed our world
we all confronted the strangely intimidating opportunity
to consume less and create more
        reluctant sports fans learned to meditate
        liberated university students became autodidacts
        skeptical concertgoers began to look within
        husbands talked with wives
        long neglected books received the attention they craved
        senseless rushing from here to nowhere ceased
        slightly less war was waged
trust was more valuable than oil

## PANDEMIC (HOW LONG)

When the pandemic paralyzed our world
we all asked ourselves
How long could you go on like this?

Perspicacious scientists observed a startling correlation
(and were careful to not call it causation)

According to the data
those of us who had neglected to develop a robust inner life
felt they might crack within twenty-four hours
crazed from a lack of external stimuli

The ones who regularly looked within
happily reported
they could go on like this
forever

## *PANDEMIC (CONNECTIONS)*

When the pandemic paralyzed our world
many of us remarked on the sublime irony
embodied in a disease capable of simultaneously keeping us apart
while bringing us closer
inspiring renewed connections
formed like neural synapses and mushroom mycelium
webbing us together in a grand tapestry
haphazardly stitched with virtual happy hours
unexpected phone calls from seldom heard friends
memories
of warmly hugging and kissing
without a care

## *PANDEMIC (POSSIBILITIES)*

When the pandemic paralyzed our world
the protracted period of enforced inactivity
allowed us all ample time to imagine our lives
post-apocalypse

Upon sincere reflection
we collectively realized our fervent wish
and ultimate goal
was for nothing to ever be
as it once was

# DEBORAH SCHMEDEMANN

## *PUZZLING*

It felt risky to be out and about that early March afternoon in 2021. My husband Craig drove; I told him the addresses and navigated. As we approached each home, I texted our friends: "Five minutes out." Most waved from a window as I dropped their brown grocery bag on their stoop; a few chatted from a safe distance. Each bag held two packages of gourmet popcorn and a jigsaw puzzle securely wrapped in brown paper with a set of instructions taped on the front.

Saturday morning, March 13, we convened on Zoom for our Pandemic Puzzle Party. Our computer screen filled with fifteen squares of couples who have gathered for years at worship and church gatherings, July Fourth picnics and New Year's Eve count-downs, dinners in our homes and theirs. We had been apart since the pandemic began.

Craig explained (most of) the contests we had devised, our friends tore open the brown paper wrapping, and the puzzle working began. We had picked a 200-piece puzzle of a silly barnyard scene with comical animals in bright colors; we hoped our friends would chuckle and finish it in forty-five minutes. A few minutes passed. More minutes passed. Craig and I munched our popcorn. We watched and wondered about our muted friends' progress. At about ten minutes, a voice came through: "We've done the border!" The first contest was complete. And indeed the other contests were completed in due time as well: the chicken's beak; the entire dog; the entire puzzle.

In this pandemic time, Craig and I are often drawn to a table strewn with petite pieces of colored cardboard. We have worked many a realistic or fanciful nature scene; idyllic village scenes; and arty composites of our home-state's symbols, Christmas wreaths, cheery images. Most resemble the picture on the box, but a few contain twists for us to discover. Our sweet spot is a rectangular 500-piece puzzle of a serene nature scene. Even with our wooden puzzle platform and its four trays into which we sort similar pieces, we generally take a few hours over a couple days to complete such a puzzle.

Craig and I have our patterns, our patter. I lay out the pieces, so I can claim the border pieces and assemble them, beads along a necklace. Meanwhile Craig assembles sections of the interior, which, best I can tell, he forms by collecting and connecting pieces with similar colors and patterns—a bird, a a window, one of the wreaths. I add pieces to my border; he makes more sections. Eventually we merge into working on zones, careful, mostly, to alert each other where we are working so as not to overlap.

Every few minutes, I opine about the puzzle (why it is more or less easy than the last one, for example) and narrate my progress (how long I have been looking for a particular piece). He is less inclined to do this. More than once per puzzle, I accuse Craig or our cat of hiding the piece I am seeking. Craig never accuses me of this offense. He is most inclined to murmur ("Got one.") or praise me ("Good job, Deborah.").

༄ ༄ ༄

Before the pandemic, working puzzles was an occasional joint hobby: a way for us to do the same thing at the same place at the same time. But then, as for so many people, the pandemic stole activities from Craig and me. Both retired, we lost volunteer work, exercise and entertainment options, socializing *with* friends, travel. Most painfully, we were stranded from our daughters' families and our extended families, who all live states away from us. We needed something to do.

As the pandemic set in and wore on, the smooth surface of our life together cracked, and cracked, and cracked again: Just a few miles from our home, George Floyd was murdered, setting off an overdue and deeply unsettling racial reckoning that reverberates still. Our beloved dog succumbed to cancer. Craig's mother (our last living parent) took her last breath half a country away. The son of friends died of suicide, out of the blue. . . . We have needed something to distract us, to settle us.

And so we have assembled jigsaw puzzles. As we study the image on the box, we slip away from our here and now and slide into the scene: a European village in pastel spring, a campground in vivid summer, a birch forest with falling snow and bright birds. As we gaze at and pick up the pieces, miniature pieces of art, each of them, our senses—sight, touch—rule our over-busy minds. I am a word person, not visually adept, so I must concentrate hard: *Is this piece the bright pink I am seeking, or is it too pale? Oh, that bisecting black line is too wide; I see that now. Is the knob I am looking for shaped like an arrow or an anchor or a ski-boot?* My mind thus engaged cannot also go into dark and sad places. And we feel accomplished, albeit in tiny ways: the border completed, Craig's section connects to my border, a piece long sought suddenly found, the last few pieces set in as we say together "Ta-dah!" Precious endorphin spurts!

As Russia invaded Ukraine, we opened a new puzzle: yellow, red, and blue birds visit a bird-feeder, shaped like a chalet and dusted with snow, leafless trees blurry in the background. A 500-piece, rectangular puzzle: our standard fare. And yet we labored to complete it. I got the border done, but the interior was vexing for both me and Craig. Were we both just so unsettled, so anguished that we were not concentrating? Should we give up? We both came to the same realization about the same time: Craig read a note on the box stating that no two pieces were identical; I figured out that I was having trouble categorizing the pieces. Oh: these puzzle pieces were not the shapes we were used to. We needed to re-frame our understanding of this puzzle.

Working puzzles has helped us re-frame our experience of this pandemic time. We have come to puzzling acutely aware of the fissures in our society and the fractures in our lives; of our lack of control over their timing, their intensity and, most painfully, their solution and their healing; of our tendency to lose ourselves to despair and sorrow. As we have worked with the petite pieces of colored cardboard strewn on our table, we have found that we can (temporarily) find ease; we can with persistence and focus make our pieces fit together; we can see our lives as cracked and yet also, reassembled, whole.

We concluded our puzzle party, held on the first anniversary of the pandemic, with one final prize, indeed the best one: given to the couple with the most pieces left to be placed in their puzzle. A finished puzzle was never the point of our party; the puzzling—together—was.

## ALISON STONE

## *WHAT IF I ADMIT I LIKE IT*

Not illness and death, of course.
Not people bankrupt and starving,
not bills and no way to pay.
Not the crisis, but the quiet—
my dog and I alone on clean dawn streets.
My teen daughters home for every meal.
Time at night to look for patterns in the stars.
Can we keep some of this when businesses open,

or will we barrel forward even faster than before
to make up for lost time?
Will the lions taking naps on roads
fade into myth along with neighbors
joined in song, the smog-gray sky
turned back to its true blue?

## *HERD*

Elk on golf courses, bears
in the streets—
with humans on lockdown,
the animals go to town.
Bright spot in the news feed's cycle
of bluster and alarm.

The virus kills by robbing oxygen
from the blood.
African Americans are dying
in higher proportions. *I can't breathe,*
Eric Garner cried. *I can't breathe,*
my client laments, trapped
24/7 with an angry, controlling spouse.
Her suffering is real, though relative.
As is shortness of breath.

With no access to salons,
our animal selves are on display—
shaggy, unwaxed, nails growing unshaped.
With rough hands, we flip from the scientists
and politicians to watch sea turtles return
unbothered, lay their eggs on beaches where
no tourists crush shells or make love.

## SHELTER IN PLACE

Crocus, snowdrop, daffodil. Expanding light.
Yards hedged by forsythia, yellow as
the Caution tape blocking off the playground.
No squeals of children, murmurings of moms.

Yards hedged by forsythia. *Yellow* as
slur—*cowardly*. Attacks on Asian-Americans.
Squeals of children, murmurings of moms
as school becomes the computer or kitchen table.

Slurs. Attacks on Asian-Americans.
There must be someone to blame.
School becomes the computer or kitchen table.
Today's lesson: fear. Tomorrow's: death.

There must be someone to blame.
Nurses wear bandanas or garbage bags.
Today's lesson: fear. Tomorrow's: death.
For distraction, we watch movies. Take walks.

Nurses wear bandanas or garbage bags.
On the news, a curve, climbing higher.
For distraction we watch movies. Takes walks,
praise what we can.

On the news, a curve climbing higher,
Caution tape blocking off playgrounds.
Still, we praise what we can—
crocus, snowdrop, daffodil. Expanding light.

# MARY E. KENDIG

## *HOW I SPENT MY PANDEMIC VACATION*

In clearing the clutter of non-essential documents from my computer srecently, I came across a piece I wrote during our Great Pandemic of 2019–2020 (still ongoing). Below are segments of my original work, each followed by a present-day reflection. It's been eye-opening for me to compare, and this has led me to understand more clearly than ever that I—and we as a people—can overcome almost anything if we approach it with patience, faith, perseverance, a little luck, and the support of those who care.

2020: *Typically, summer is a carefree time of year. A season during which friends and family text and tweet about, and post photo collages of, their journeys to beautiful places as they while away their summer breaks soaking up the sun and leaving their worries aside.*

*But this year, things are different. Because this is the summer of Covid-19—a summer during which the prospect of carefree days has been tossed to the virus-laden wind, replaced by the devastating dilemma of the here and now.*

*On March 23, 2020, because of this pandemic, I was furloughed from my job, along with a record thirty million people in the US who have been laid off or furloughed because of the Covid-19 pandemic. This marked the first time in forty-six years of toiling in Corporate America that I had ever been let go of a job. It's a humbling, awful "first" for me and so many others. And it's quite demoralizing to know that I am now but a sad statistic in the midst of an overwhelming sea of statistics, through no fault of my own.*

*I began my unemployment after years of intense, stress-filled dedication to my demanding but apparently non-essential job as a print production manager for a large restaurant chain. I mentioned rather pointedly to my boss during one of our last calls that I felt there was a reason the word furlough began with an F-U.*

*Living in this horrible, suspended state of hopeless uncertainty is like living in that proverbial van down by the river, with four flat tires, no gas, no cell phone, and no way to get out, all the while watching the rains pour and realizing that* the currents will change and the river will soon rise to unprecedented flood levels. And, because you've lost your voice, no one can hear you screaming.

2022: In some ways, I'm still not over being let go from a job I felt I did exceedingly well. But in the long run, I'm seeing my unceremonious heave-ho as a blessing, because I'm now in better control of my health. For one, my stress-induced perpetually high blood pressure isn't so high anymore. I'm taking one less prescription pill. And my dentist says that my gums have never looked better. I told him that's probably because I have more time to brush my teeth now. My prior mention of living in a "horrible, suspended state of hopeless uncertainty" has now turned into a hopeful, cautious, yet slow transition into retirement. Actually, living simply in that van down by the river sounds quite relaxing to me now, cell phones and flood waters be damned.

2020: *Having to file for unemployment compensation alongside hundreds of thousands of others at the same time is a living nightmare. And we endure this anguish for the privilege (in my case) of collecting $275 a week, for just twelve weeks. Luckily, I had fifteen vacation days stashed from which I could collect pay before filing. But many didn't—and don't—have that cushion.*

2022: I consider myself fortunate in that, after a wait of about two months for benefits to begin, the much-maligned unemployment compensation system didn't forget me (although I am sorrowfully aware that this was not the case for many). I received my benefits as expected and continued to receive unemployment compensation for longer than twelve weeks, thanks to government-provided stimulus monies and extended relief over the rest of 2020 and into 2021. That offered me a much-needed initial sigh of relief and made me realize that maybe I could get through this ordeal. Granted, I was fortunate to have had enough savings to help me along. I was luckier than many others.

2020: *Since March 23 I've slowly become an insomniac, with no ability to sleep through the night. Case in point: I'm writing this on a Sunday at 2:23 a.m., when most others are likely at rest. But not me. When your career, salary, healthcare coverage, and future well-being, not to mention the health and safety of your country and the entire world, are in limbo, your sleep pattern, along with your positive outlook, are pretty much shot to smithereens.*

2022: I've been sleeping well enough these days and enjoying the extra time to rest, especially in the mornings. And I've discovered the supreme joy of the afternoon nap. After forty-six years of rising before dawn and trudging my way to jobs at least an hour away, I can finally relax. Healthcare worries were also resolved because I was able to enroll in coverage through the Affordable Care Act. And, most important of all, I've come to realize that my career was not my life. My family and friends and wonderful shared experiences are my life. And I'm happy to say I've got more time for those things—the things that truly count.

2020: *Searching the web for new recipes that could help lift my mood and stretch a dollar, I found a great (and apropos) one for "depression cake," which contains no milk, no eggs, and no butter but results in a rather moist and enjoyable chocolate cake. (Not surprisingly, chocolate cake has become essential to me of late.) The recipe calls for apple cider vinegar, oil, vanilla and water, and of course flour, sugar, unsweetened cocoa powder, and baking soda. It's easy to make, and it's versatile because you can substitute items to create new variations. For instance, I omitted the cocoa powder and water and subbed in a can of creamed corn to make the best cornbread I've tasted in a while. Creating this simple concoction has boosted my spirits and has shown me that I can adapt and still be inspired if I put my mind to it. Those little things mean a lot, especially given the current situation.*

2022: Our rapid-onset, rising inflation has me still trying hard to stretch a dollar, but I don't make depression cake any longer. Upon reflection, I never really liked it as much as I initially let on. I have, though, moved on to indulge my interest in cooking. I like simple, easy recipes the best, and I've come to realize that I have a knack for this stuff, and people seem to enjoy what I create.

2020: *Seeing repeated warnings that my "storage space is almost full," I wrestled with my Samsung cell phone, finally figuring out how to de-clutter it. After two full weeks of clearing caches, deleting histories and files (I deleted many of my favorite pictures and text messages), and running device scans and reboots, all the while pacing to and fro in the living room trying to come to grips with how to approach this dilemma, I managed to win at something, thanks in no small part to the tips I found on the internet, which does sometimes come through in a pinch. Yay, YouTube. Yay, me.*

2022: I'm now a 5G phone owner, and I have no issues with phone-related clutter at the moment. I've also slowly begun to de-clutter more than just my cell phone. My closets and kitchen cabinets have never been more organized, and it's felt freeing to wade through and donate a lot of things that I'd hung onto for far too long.

2020: *Approaching our sixth week together in isolation, I began to invent endearing new nicknames for my spouse. The most effective of these was "Mount Etna," relating to his penchant for eruption of the verbal sort in response to the little things that often go awry, like there being no pull tab on the can of cashew nuts. "Oh, damn it!" I heard him exclaim one evening, to which I replied, "Oh my God, what's wrong?" To which he answered, "There's no pull tab on the can of cashew nuts!" Heavens, I thought to myself. How can we possibly live another day?*

*And that is just the kind of absurd overreaction you have during a pandemic. Because of the unnerving helplessness you feel, punctuated each evening on hearing the frightening number of daily dead announced on the evening news. And you already know that your age, and your underlying health conditions, and your blood type, and countless other things, put you in a high-risk group. And you fervently do hope you can live another day. And then you come to your senses and you vow that you will never again, if you have a breath of life left in you once this nightmare is over, complain about inane little things like the lack of a pull tab on your can of cashew nuts. At least you can still afford the cashew nuts. And a comfortable home in which to eat them. For now.*

2022: "Mount Etna" seems to be relatively quiet of late, so that nickname has become obsolete, gone the proverbial way of the dodo. We still enjoy cashew nuts, but not as often (because they are quite pricey). And delightfully, we seem to have moved on from overreacting to things like the absence of pull tabs. We have kept our vow. There are more important things worthy of our worry, such as the brutalities of war and human suffering and hunger, and about those things we still do worry and care deeply and try to do something. And, most especially, we simply rejoice in being alive and healthy and in still being able to occasionally afford and enjoy a serving of cashew nuts. Two relatively contented nuts in a cashew pod are we, all things considered.

2020: *I finally started working on a new children's book—and I finished it. This took me fifteen years, as my first book was written in the good old pre-pandemic days of 2005. Several friends had encouraged me to write another kids' book. But I had never taken them up on it, thinking that I didn't have a good enough idea—that is, until I was persuaded to get busy doing something by virtue of my new, unemployed, mostly home-confined status. And by the unexpected motivation given to me by a three-year-old wonder named Charlotte, whose dad had been reading my first book to her every evening because that book was one of her favorites. Buoyed by that lovely three-year-old motivator, my second book came together quickly, and it helped me to remember that I can also create some decent book illustrations as well. I plan to publish it next year, when (most hopefully) the world is closer to being its old self again.*

2022: I found a local book publisher, and I published that second book. I completed another project that I was proud of! Turns out, kids are enjoying my second book, too, along with my first, and that simple fact makes it all worthwhile. This was never an endeavor meant to turn a profit; it was a project from the heart meant to bring a little joy to kids. Charlotte and the other children who've read my book seem to like it a lot, and it's also brought me joy. And that, to me, is the essence of success.

⚜ ⚜ ⚜

2020: *All of my self-centered babble aside, the most horrifying aspect of this entire period is having to cope with the risk of falling ill with or dying from Covid-19, the most aggressive virus the world has seen since 1918. Never have we been so apprehensive about doing the most mundane things, like going to the grocery store, or filling a gas tank, or getting within six feet of another human. But this is a strange world we're living in.*

*And, on a daily basis in this strange world, I find myself moved to tears upon seeing the selfless sacrifice of so many doctors, nurses and hospital staff. I am in awe of the devoted workers who help the lonely, isolated seniors in our nursing homes. And I am overwhelmingly proud of the gutsy grocery store employees, truckers, restaurant staff, and farm workers who are making sure our country keeps going. I'm deeply moved by so many others, too—and by the pain experienced by the families of those who have died. And I am worried for the homeless and for all those less fortunate. I am also frustrated beyond measure that I'm not equipped to do more to help. A few small things I am doing, however, are contributing dry and canned goods regularly to my local food bank, volunteering to review and edit resumes for others in search of work, following the science and all the rules, and trying to educate those in my corner of the pandemic world who refuse to follow those rules. And I'm praying for all of us. Praying that the Lord will help us to overcome this deadly plague, because this mind-numbing global predicament is still months, perhaps years away from being over.*

*Dear scientists, I am pulling for you with every fiber of my non-essential being to resolve this crisis. I, a fellow nerd, admire and respect you. All of us deeply, most sincerely appreciate you. And we hope you can come up with—quickly, we pray—the vaccine or vaccines that will obliterate this mysterious, deadly virus forever so that we boring, imperfect, chocolate-cake-eating regular folk can return to our mundane but normal existences, and our perfectly normal summers, and maybe even our regular jobs, without the current wave of dread that is alive among us. Please and thank you. Amen.*

2022: I'll say it again—I have survived, maybe even thrived, and I am lucky. And vaccinated and boosted, thanks to the scientists and researchers with whom we're fortunate enough to share our imperfect world. I still have my chronic aches and pains, though overall I am healthy, along with my spouse. We sometimes get on each other's nerves, mostly because we're spending gobs more time together, but we are working through the rough stuff and trying to find some joy in the everyday. I am still apprehensive about the future, unsure of whether I am really, truly financially and physically prepared for it.

Psychologically and emotionally, however, I'm okay with where I am, looking forward to having time to enjoy more things, big and small (but mostly small) in the time I have left. I still see things happening in today's world that are vicious and cruel and alarming. But I am trying to be strong and optimistic, to be helpful and humble, and to act as a positive force to the extent that I can. I try to put a little joy back into this world, by writing my little books for kids, by helping my neighbors and my family and friends, by being a good person and a good citizen. And I continue to pray for all of us.

These days, I'm slowly moving beyond the dread I felt two years ago and stepping out onto the ledge of anticipation for the future. And that transition has been aided, in no small measure, by taking the time to pause and reflect—to be thankful that I am not alone and to rejoice in knowing that I have been patient, have endured and persevered, and have powered through.

## KRISTY SNEDDEN

### *DANCING WITH VIRGINIA*

Virginia asked for a poem
about John Lewis.
See my heart,
its recent fortitude leaks.

I type lines on my laptop to bear it.
This curious mix, racism and joie de vivre.
I'm looking at a crowd of people, dancing.
I text lines to my own phone

while the same poem writes itself
on my iPad, Microsoft privilege.
The crowd is every color. The poetry
shapes Virginia's face, etches her hope

until it is the grand jete, from her eyes to mine. We were
Duo-ing, step-touch, pivot/turn, still she gathered my tears,
cocooned them in her own chasse, then handed
them back with graceful precision and whispered

the Statesman's words, "Settle down now." "Keep moving forward."
If he was here, I'd tell him about the crowd dancing together, every shade,
each nationality, slow dancing to Bob Marley's *Redemption Song*
and he would laugh and pull me in, saying, "Be of Good Courage."

Then I would find myself, back in a church
meeting room, not all colors, but more than a few.
We were open for blessings. His voice rang like bells
in my body, found a home in my oxygen.

"Settle Down Now. Be Of Good Courage. Keep Moving Forward."

## *KUDZU*

You seemed distracted
Saturday, your colors off.
I struggled to pray.

At the haunted lake,
ancestors in finery
danced between the trees.

Kudzu lurked, creeping
over monuments hiding
crimes some won't confess.

Since then, we lost ten
more bodies we can't bury.
Covid's rolling spikes.

DC welcomed troops
to camp in the Capital.
I didn't dream that

Warnock, the preacher,
studious in his glasses,
went to the District.

John Lewis is dead.
The son of sharecroppers said,
"Get in good trouble,"

but the capitol
seems empty, with its armed guards.
I keep losing you.

When I tell you this
in foreign languages, you
always say, "I'm here."

## NICHOLAS SAMARAS

*JOURNAL IN THE PLAGUE YEAR*

*1. Every New Year Always Begins in Innocence*

Each January starts fresh with anticipation, resolution,
and swells into its own wake of sameness.

Entering the most recent plague year was equally ordinary
with nobody thinking anything beyond themselves—

the cold month and what coldness brings:
the flu season when people walk around with February faces.

Mid-January was publicly uneventful
with our preoccupied heads down to the face of the world,

the news merely an assortment of rumors
from other countries, and nobody lifted their heads—

much like the way war is:
always abstract and amorphous

until war touches you personally—
and then it becomes real.

*2. Distant Thunder*

The ordinary days continued that way
from January into February, the volume of reports

beginning to rise. By earliest March,
the static of the news became a loud buzzing

with the numbers of deaths always in some other country—
and nobody we knew.

*3. The Ides of March*

In the plague year,
overnight, there was suddenly no other news but this.

In the plague year,
we learned the term "coronavirus,"—not bubonic, but "novel."

In the plague year,
locked down, all we could do was look around stunned.

In the plague year,
I sat in my back yard and lifted my face to the warm sun.

In the plague year,
I sat there hourly, listening intently to the wind.

In the plague year,
I sat on the deck facing out to my back yard

and stared lovingly into the trees,
their dense and healthy foliage.

In the plague year,
everything was normal until everything wasn't.

*4. I Loved the Poetry of the Pandemic*

At least, I actually loved the poetry of the pandemic—
the phraseology of a virus shaped like a crown of colorful jewels,

to look over our rising horizon
and enter the land of social distancing, to even love

the music of that phrase—to regard the newness of words
in their turning context, to "shelter in place"

and be comforted by the new idea of home—
for me to stay domestic on Mandarin Lane in West Nyack,

in a spacious greenery, the forested nature
twenty miles north of Manhattan, to regard

the music and safety of my address. At least,
we still had shelter, we were not coughing, and society

had not collapsed overnight. At least, we were still
with our families. For the initial days, we were

only inconvenienced, helping to "flatten the curve."
Our lives, still nothing like the old saints

torn and rendered apart. We were still
only in the land of the bothered

and death happened to other people in other countries
or in the county next to ours, skirting closer.

## 5. April as Depth

My wife lost her job. My daughter lost
her job and her apartment. I read Daniel Dafoe's plague book,

whose uncle worked as a saddler—the same job as my grandfather
who survived the American Spanish Influenza a hundred years ago.

My multiple jobs stitched together to let me work "remotely"
for a continued paycheck and survival. And we were only

two weeks in, then three weeks in, a month of strangeness
in which the healthy were quarantined. After days, I felt dizzy,

a temptation to dizziness until I pushed it away,
thinking it's only psychological. When I went to bed tired

and woke up exhausted, I thought—only psychological.
Until the numbers crept closer to us, daily. Until we woke

to find ourselves the world's new epicenter of the pandemic—
with the highest number of deaths. Until we became numb

with death becoming a daily headcount, ascending exponentially.
A two-week stretch in April and then the days lost count—

losing track of which day it was, the only count becoming
how many died yesterday: in New York City, eight hundred people

dying per day. Until we realized now that everything is personal—
whereas before, if something wasn't personal, it didn't exist.

What is both so ancient and contemporary as a plague?
Perversely, I read and watched histories of epidemics and contagion.

I marveled at the surprise of it, as if all this had never
happened before, when it's now happening to you.

*6. The Novelty of Masks*

Citizens of Japan wore masks in public from years ago.
I remember the photographs and thinking, how insane

the smog that bad. Now, welcome to their world.
When the blue and white surgical masks ran out,

we used long handkerchiefs, me wearing
my college bandana across my nose and mouth.

At my bank, withdrawing savings, I said,
"Give me all your money"—and nobody laughed.

The only deposit we had was humor.
At the grocery store, the long lines waiting outside—

one person let in to shop, after one person came out.
No disinfectants to be found.

People fighting over toilet paper.
Shelves empty of basics.

All the complacent years before, with the popular movies
of the "zombie apocalypse" and various doomsdays,

we never thought of what would become deemed
essential or superfluous.

The mask felt like suffocating, muffled and rasping,
but I bowed to courtesy, participating in the "greater good."

Claustrophobic and breathing heavy,
I wore that mask for living.

*7. The Concept of World-Travel*

Earth was closed.
Airlines and hotels shut down.

National borders forbidden.
I thought of Greece—with one of the world's

lowest infection rates, having closed early in austerity.
I thought of all the countries I used to live in.

All of it became the truth of human nature—
restriction and reaction.

I was always an indoor cat,
never thinking to actually go outside

until we were told to stay at home.
After that, all I wanted to do

was walk outside in skylight and oxygen.
Amazing to want something

only when we're told
we can't have it.

8. *Great Lent in the Pandemic*

It was funny to read what our Western society deemed
"essential" workers and "non-essential" workers—

with alcohol stores kept open and churches closed.
It was funny to read how authorities started

arresting priests who kept their churches open—
until we all stayed home and "live-streamed" our prayers.

I thought of fasting as part of a greater
obedience, patience, and compassion for others.

Without that, I thought physical fasting was pointless.
All I could do, then, was use the pandemic to practice

the true meaning of fasting and Great Lent, praying
for minor resurrections. And like eternity, time slowed down.

I passed the trudging weeks by reading critics of the "sheeple"
who followed whatever was told, the flying counter-arguments

of conspiracies. I saw videos of my beloved Pacific
and thought of how to swim in a hazmat suit.

In the beginning, it was all novel and unreal.
I loved the social distancing—to see how finally

my introverted lifestyle gained street-credibility.
In the middle, hospitals wouldn't even test you for the virus

unless you were showing symptoms.
In the middle, it took two weeks to get test results back.

When the ventilators ran out, people died faster
and we couldn't attend the funerals. By then,

forty days was an eternity, the most bitter test
of faith and patience to slowly turn into endurance.

*9. Time Without Days or Counting*

First, only the elderly died.
Weeks into the epidemic, the first baby died.

After that, every age died indiscriminately.
We noticed to question why ethnic and lower-economic groups

died in exponentially higher numbers.
Still in April, the world's viral count passed its first million,

reminding us we were still part of the world.
Photographs in the city showed hospitals overwhelmed,

bodies piled up inside morgue refrigeration trucks—
the white sheets, the black bags stacked like cordwood.

When funerals were allowed again, we waited
two hours in our cars, just to get into the cemetery gates.

Otherwise, we stayed in our homes and counted
the dead, commemorating the ones we knew.

Even our first responders got the virus, with reports
of doctors and nurses committing suicide.

Without garbage from humans, even the city rats
began to starve and attack each other.

My mind said to leave a record for the generations,
write any of this down to remember what our lives

used to be like, what our lives were becoming.
For my children, I suited up in my mask, my filmy gloves,

and risked driving out to buy groceries for another month,
to live that long for as long as possible.

*10. "The Human Pause"*

By May, through my front window, I spent long days,
watching strangers in my neighborhood

stroll the empty streets—clusters of small families walking
slightly apart from other clusters of small families.

Slowly, my neighborhood of West Nyack tinged
green with nature, red robins nesting in my deck rafters.

In our closed isolation, we watched the photographic news
from people who ventured out to witness small miracles—

how the world comes back without us.
Animals took over the world's vacant streets:

the fallow deer grazing in Foxton park, my birth-home
of 4 Dryden Cottage, eight miles south of Cambridge, England—

videos of pumas cautiously encroaching
back into the streets of Santiago, Chile,

mountain goats clipping over the lanes of Powys, Wales,
my other old home—and bears nosing through my old village

of Kosovo, most everywhere I ever lived the world over.
Even the sight of Mount Everest finally became visible again

from a hundred miles away in Kathmandu, Nepal—the pure air
blue and crystalline. And the space station astronauts

being able to look down and see the Earth clearly,
after our worst century of pollution.

For us to perceive how this earth may revive without us,
how the earth comes back after the virus of humanity.

*11. In the Fourth Month of the Pandemic*

Still, the spring air held onto its coldness for a long time
into the reluctant June summer. By then, we thought

of the virus as atmosphere, and got on with our numberless
days, our attentions turned to other news, regular news:

the ongoing and ancient, the deaths of black citizens by police
for no legal reason:  otherwise known as Friday.

The ancient and ongoing reports of police
killing black people sleeping in their beds, or out jogging,

driving their cars, standing in public, buying anything.
Until we realized, after centuries and reams of lynched names,

it was never the Coronavirus we had to fear.
It was racism that was the greater virus—always with us,

infecting our long history, the American caste system.
Until this was the newest tipping point. Until the new protests

swelled to a fever-pitch, the peaceful mobs marching for justice,
infiltrators goading for power, police kettling, the riots and looting.

While the now-named Covid-19 virus was killing us
indiscriminately, objectively, equally—we continued

killing each other selectively and completely discriminately.
I thought again of the white shrouds, the black bags—

the piling up of humanity like neat garbage. With the mattering
of black lives and my cheering the dismantling of confederate bigotry,

all I could pray for was the smoke of the world to lift
out of this world and dissipate into a Heaven we can breathe in.

*12. Coda*

Edging into summer and past summer, ten million infected,
half a million dead—I saw how the virus hit everyone

except politicians at their election rallies
and celebrities sheltering in place in their mansions,

how the lockdown lasted only as long as the economy
could hold—only as long as the price of a life was still valued

more than economy. I lost two of my jobs
when my universities lost millions and couldn't hire me back.

I took long days to repair my home and waited for news
of the virus' second wave—third wave—its inevitable coming.

By November, forty-six million infected, one million dead.
I realized how old I feel now. Seeing how the body can go

wrong at any second, I prayed to love the wind
while it was still a friend to us. I wanted to throw the log of my life

back onto the fire and, in the very end, be able to write in Heaven,
to have this be my last prayer to the blue air, the final health.

How long now may this journal last? Maybe only as long
as I may last. Maybe as long as the world stays slumbering

into a revived green, to say we were the virus, we were
the chorus of discordance—and only calamity forced us

to harmonize a final song of humanity—to say we held to patience,
to a last compassion, that we worked together to stay present tense,

to put ourselves in place by not thinking of ourselves

but of each other, to be true—that, no matter how long

virus, illness, and plagues were with us, we could hold
each other up and say, we come through, we come through.

## Acknowledgments

Kevin Brown's "Saving the Music" previously appeared in *Johnny America*.

Patricia Cannon's "Between The Silences" was initially published by the Grief Rites Foundation.

Kathie Giorgio's "Sitting" originally appeared in *Edify Publications* (April 2017).

A portion of "Only Now" by Stephanie Hart was previously published in "The Eternal Now" in *Mirror Mirror: A Collection of Memoir and Stories*.

Michael Hettich's "The River" previously appeared in *Split Rock Review* (Winter 2022).

Richard LeBlond's "The Natural Moment" first appeared in *Visitant Literary Journal* (2017).

"T'ai Chi Time" by Randy Minnich was previously published in *Potter's Wheel* (2016).

Nicholas Samaras previously published "Journal in the Plague Year" in *American Journal of Poetry* (January, 2021).

Sherry Shahan's "Loitering" originally appeared in *Trampoline Poetry* (2020).

Patty Somlo's "Raisins" was previously published in *Halfway Down the Stairs* in 2018 and again in 2020 in its fiftieth publication/milestones issue.

Allison Stone's "What if I Admitted I Like It" first appeared in the anthology *A 21st Century Plague: Poetry from a Pandemic*.

Images by Heather Tosteson. Many thanks to the contributors, family, friends and passers-by who contributed images to art with no idea what was coming next.

Members of the Wising Up Writers Collective Editorial Group—Kerry Langan, Michele Markarian, William Cass and Felicia Mitchell—provided invaluable assistance in bringing this anthology to print. We could never do what we do without them.

# Contributors

**Laura Apol** is an award-winning poet and the author of five full-length collections, most recently, *A Fine Yellow Dust*. A professor at Michigan State University and past poet laureate of Lansing, MI, Laura conducts creative writing workshops internationally, nationally, and locally.

**Lenore Balliro** lives in Gloucester, MA. She has been published in the *Atlanta Review*, *Minnesota Review*, *Louisville Review*, and several other journals and anthologies. She is a previous recipient of the RI State Council on the Arts award for literature and a winner of the Gloucester Writers Center Bianchini award.

**Mark Barkawitz** has earned multiple awards for his work in multiple genres. He has IMDb feature film credits for *Turn of the Blade* (Mark Bark) and *The Killing Time*. He lives with his wife and has two, grown children in Pasadena, CA. His critically-acclaimed new novels, *Full Moon Saturday Night* and *Feeling Lucky: A Pandemic Novel*, are now available.

**Lois Baer Barr** is a literacy tutor in Chicago. Thrice nominated for a Pushcart, Barr was a finalist for the Rita Dove Poetry Prize. Her chapbook *Biopoesis* won Poetica's first prize, and *Tracks: Poems on the "L"* is forthcoming at Finishing Line Press. During pauses, she bikes with husband Lew, walks with their Golden Doodle Aggie, and dances flamenco.

**Gaylord Brewer** is the author of sixteen books of poems, fiction, criticism, and cookery, most recently the poetry collections *The Feral Condition* (Negative Capability) and *Worship the Pig* (Red Hen). The pieces in this anthology are taken from a collection of flash non-fiction, *Before the Storm Takes It Away*, forthcoming from Red Hen in spring 2024.

**Kevin Brown** has published two short story collections, *Death Roll* and *Ink On Wood*, and has had fiction, non-fiction and poetry published in over two hundred literary journals, magazines and anthologies. He won numerous writing competitions, fellowships, and grants, and was nominated for multiple prizes and awards, including three *Pushcart Prizes*.

**Wendy Brown-Báez** is the author of *Heart on the Page: A Portable Writing Workshop*, the novel *Catch a Dream*, and two books of poetry. Her poetry and prose appear in numerous literary journals and anthologies. Wendy leads writing for healing workshops in community spaces, such as prisons, libraries, and healing centers.

**Patricia Cannon** has been a registered nurse at UCSF since 2001. She has worked in cardiac critical care, neurointensive care, hemeoncology, school nursing and, currently, in research. Her passion is her faith, photography, and the written word in all its forms. Her poetry has appeared in several magazines and books.

**Bonni Chalkin** is a Reiki master, certified meditation teacher, intuitive healer, artist, and writer. Her work has been published in anthologies by Wising Up Press, as well as *And Then* magazine. Her paintings have sold in various countries. She is passionate about helping people embrace their power and follow their intuition. She is currently working on a book of essays.

**Beth Christensen** is a psychotherapist in New Orleans. While she has enjoyed writing for years, she decided that sixty-three was a good age to start seriously pursuing publication of short fiction and creative non-fiction. She has most recently published stories in *Avalon Review; Children, Churches, and Daddies;* and the *Adult Children* anthology from Wising Up Press.

**Terry Dalrymple's** books of fiction include *Dancing on Barbed Wire* (co-authored), *Love Stories (Sort Of)*, *Texas 5X5: Twenty-Five Stories by Five Texas Writers* (co-authored), *Salvation* (stories), and *Fishing for Trouble* (novel for middle readers), as well as a book of stories he edited, *Texas Soundtrack: Texas Stories Inspired by Texas Music*. A member of the Texas Institute of Letters, he lives in San Angelo where he enjoys writing, gardening, and taking photographs.

**Diane Elayne Dees** is the author of the chapbooks, *Coronary Truth* (Kelsay Books) and *The Last Time I Saw You* (Finishing Line Press). Diane, who lives in Covington, LA, also publishes "Women Who Serve," a blog that delivers news and commentary on women's professional tennis throughout the world.

**Edward A. Dougherty** is author of eleven poetry collections, the most recent of which are *10048* (the zip code of the World Trade Center) and *Grace Street*. His latest book, *Journey Work: Crafting a Life of Poetry & Spirit,* includes essays about ripening as a poet, spiritual seeking, and peacemaking as a volunteer in Hiroshima. Granted the SUNY Chancellor's Award for Scholarship and Creative Activities, Dougherty lives in upstate New York near the convergence of three rivers.

**Chris Ellery** is the author of five poetry collections, including *The Big Mosque of Mercy*, *Elder Tree*, and, most recently, *Canticles of the Body*. A member of the Texas Institute of Letters, he has received the X.J. Kennedy Award for Creative Nonfiction, the Dora and Alexander Raynes Prize for Poetry, the Betsy Colquitt Award, and the Texas Poetry Award.

**Kathie Giorgio** is the author of six novels, two story collections, three poetry books, and an essay collection. Her novel, *All Told,* was released in January 2022, and a poetry chapbook, *Olivia In Five, Seven, Five; Autism In Haiku,* in August. Her stories/poems appeared in hundreds of magazines. She's the director/founder of AllWriters' Workplace & Workshop LLC.

**Stephanie Hart** is the author of the book *Mirror Mirror: A Collection of Memoirs and Stories* (And Then Press) as well as a young adult fiction novel. Her work has appeared in anthologies, such as *Adult Children* (Wising Up Press), and literary magazines, including *The Sun, Jewish Currents, And Then,* and *Home Plant News*.

**Nadel Henville** is a recent graduate of Emmanuel College in Boston, MA. She immigrated from St. Lucia with her family, finding a home within Connecticut. She's found a love of writing for all mediums, whether that's screenwriting, playwriting, or novels. She can always be found with a pen in her hand and her mind going a mile a minute.

**Michael Hettich** has published a dozen books, most recently *The Mica Mine,* which won the 2020 Lena Shull Book Award from the North Carolina Poetry Society. A "new and selected" volume is forthcoming from Press 53. His work has appeared in such journals as *Orion, Ploughshares, TriQuarterly Poetry East* and *The Sun*. He lives with his family in Black Mountain, NC.

**Leonore Hildebrandt** is the author of *Where You Happen to Be*, *The Next Unknown*, and *The Work at Hand*. Her poems and translations have appeared in the *Cafe Review*, *Cerise Press*, *Harpur Palate*, *Rhino*, and the *Sugar House Review*, among other journals. Leonore lives "off the grid" in Harrington, ME and spends the winter in Silver City, NM.

**Paul Hostovsky** is the author of twelve books of poetry, most recently, *Mostly* (FutureCycle Press). His poems have won a Pushcart Prize, two Best of the Net Awards, the FutureCycle Poetry Book Prize, and have been featured on Poetry Daily, Verse Daily, and The Writer's Almanac. He has also been a featured poet on the Georgia Poetry Circuit. He makes his living in Boston as a sign language interpreter.

**Tony Hozeny** is author of the novels *Driving Wheel* and *My House Is Dark* and numerous short stories. He has an MFA from Johns Hopkins and taught creative writing at four colleges. Over the past two years, he has placed ten stories in literary magazines. Three of the stories have been anthologized.

**Mary Jumbelic** has published her creative nonfiction stories with *Rutgers University Press*, *Tortoise and Finch*, *Foliate Oak Literary Magazine*, *Vine Leaves Press*, *GFT Press*, *Women on Writing*, *Jelly Bucket*, *Closed Eye Open*, *Prometheus Dreaming*, *Grapple Alley*, *Change Seven*, *Dreamers Creative Writing*, *Hektoen*, *Sterling Clack Clack*, *Free Spirit*, *Griffel*, *Unleash Press*, *Humans of the World*, *Write Launch*, and *Multiplicity*.

**Murali Kamma** is the author of *Not Native: Short Stories of Immigrant Life in an In-Between World* (Wising Up Press), which won an Independent Publisher Book Award. His stories have appeared in *Havik*, *Evening Street Review*, *Rosebud*, etc. He contributes to *New York Journal of Books*, and his fiction was included in *The Best Asian Short Stories* and other anthologies.

**Mary E. Kendig** authored and illustrated the children's books *Wonderful Words: Fun Poems About Words* and its sequel. She has served as a guest editor for Southern New Hampshire University's online literary journal, *The Penman Review*. Mary is a contributing writer in a short-story anthology entitled *Letters to Loved Ones: A Journey Through Grief* and in *Goodness* (Wising Up Press).

**Laurie Klein** is the author of a poetry collection, *Where the Sky Opens* (Poeima/ Cascade), and an award-winning chapbook, *Bodies of Water, Bodies of Flesh*. Her work has appeared or is forthcoming in *Brevity, Beautiful Things, Eco-Theo, New Letters, Cold Mountain Review, Louisiana Literature, Ars Medica, Tiferet,* and elsewhere.

**Richard LeBlond** is a retired biologist living in North Carolina. His essays and photographs have appeared in many U.S. and international journals, including *Montreal Review, Weber—The Contemporary West, Concis, Lowestoft Chronicle, Trampset,* and *Still Point Arts Quarterly*. His work has been nominated for "Best American Travel Writing" and "Best of the Net."

**Larry Lefkowitz** has had published over 150 stories, as well as poetry and humor books. His Jewish story collection, *Enigmatic Tales*, was published by Fomite Press, which will also publish his new novella and story collection *Lefkowitz Unbound*.

**Arlene Gay Levine** is the author of *39 Ways to Open Your Heart: An Illuminated Meditation* (Conari Press) and *Movie Life* (Finishing Line Press). Her prose and poetry have found a home in the *New York Times*, numerous anthologies, online and in journals including *Chiron Review, MacGuffin,* and *Frogpond*.

**Russ Allison Loar's** writing has appeared in the anthology *Heart Of A Man, Bryant Literary Review, High Shelf Press, Bright Flash Literary Review, Abstract Magazine, Evening Street Review, Coffin Bell Journal* and *Ravens Perch*. Loar has a degree in journalism and has written news and feature stories for newspapers including the *Los Angeles Times*.

**Randy Minnich** is a retired chemistry professor and researcher. He has published two books, *Wildness in a Small Place* and *Pavlov's Cats, Their Story*. His poetry has appeared in *Blueline, Main Street Rag, U.S. 1 Worksheets, Uppagus,* and other publications.

**MK Punky**, author of thirteen books of fiction, memoir and journalism, is the creator of *The Year of When*, a 365-poem multi-media exhibition about 2020. A frequent contributor to Wising Up Press, MK serves as poet laureate of the Vista Street Community Library in Los Angeles.

**Laura Redford** has a BS from Central Missouri University. Her short stories have been published in three anthologies; *Kaleidoscope WoJo, Chicken Soup For the Soul* and *More Voices of the Willows*. She also has self-published a historical novel: *Where Roses Grow* under her author's name, Laura Lewis.

**Molly Rivkin** is a poet, outdoor enthusiast, yogini, and whitewater raft guide. She is a passionate writer, and most enjoys creating spoken word poetry and memoir. Her first novel, *Tea Without Vodka is a Son of a Bitch*, is joyfully waiting to be published and read.

**James Silas Rogers** is the author of two poetry collections, *Sundogs* and *The Collector of Shadows*, as well as an essay collection about cemeteries, *Northern Orchards: Places Near the Dead*. Four of his pieces have been selected as "notables" in the annual *Best American Essays* volumes. He has also published widely on Irish writing.

**Mary Kay Rummel's** ninth poetry book, *Nocturnes: Between Flesh and Stone*, has recently been published by Blue Light Press. Her first book, *This Body She's Entered*, won a Minnesota Voices Award from New Rivers Press. *The Lifeline Trembles* won the Blue Light Award. She is poet laureate emerita of Ventura County, CA and divides her time between Minneapolis and Ventura.

**Nicholas Samaras** is the author of *Hands of the Saddlemaker* (Yale University Press) and *American Psalm, World Psalm* (Ashland). He is currently completing a manuscript of poetry on California and a memoir of his childhood lived underground.

**Richard Schiffman** is an environmental reporter, poet and author of two biographies. His poems have appeared in the *Alaska Quarterly, New Ohio Review, Christian Science Monitor, New York Times, Writer's Almanac, This American Life in Poetry, Verse Daily* and other publications. His first poetry collection *What the Dust Doesn't Know* was published in 2017 (Salmon Poetry).

**Deborah Schmedemann** has been writing personal essays since retiring from her career as a law professor and lawyer. Her essays appear in print and online publications including two anthologies published by Wising Up

Press: *Surprised by Joy* and *Adult Children*. With Covid easing, she is thrilled to return to in-person teaching of adult English language learners, tutoring young readers, and visiting her daughters' families.

**Sherry Shahan** lives in a laid-back beach town in California. Her poetry has appeared in *F(r)iction, Trampoline Poetry, Herstry, Oyster River, Goats Milk, Odyssey* and is forthcoming from *Impspired*. She earned an MFA from Vermont College of Fine Arts and taught a creative writing course for UCLA Extension for ten years.

**Sharon D. Sheltzer,** recently retired architect, penned this essay about deconstructing her house, opposite of what she usually does with houses. She has turned her love of the creative process to writing, and as an indie author published a memoir, *Woman Overboard: A Splash of Insight into Sleep Deprivation and Psychosis.* She is presently working on a novel.

**Laura Shovan** is an educator, award-winning children's novelist, and Pushcart Prize-nominated poet. Her chapbook, *Mountain, Log, Salt, and Stone* won the inaugural Harriss Poetry Prize. Laura's work appears in many journals and anthologies for children and adults. She teaches for Vermont College of Fine Arts' MFA in Writing for Children and Young Adults.

**Zoe Singer** holds degrees in English literature from the University of Michigan and Breadloaf School of English. She has attended poetry workshops at the New School and read her work on *Morning Edition* for WNYC. She works as a senior grant writer at Planned Parenthood Federation of America, and lives in Brooklyn with her son.

**Claude Clayton Smith** is the author of eight books and co-editor/translator of four others. His own work has been translated into five languages, including Russian and Chinese. His degrees include an MFA in fiction from the Writers' Workshop at the University of Iowa. His short story "Helping Padraig Die" won the 2021 Great Midwest Fiction Contest of *Midwest Review*.

**Kristy Snedden** has been a trauma psychotherapist for thirty-plus years. Her work appears/is forthcoming in *Amethyst Review; Book of Matches; Poetry Super Highway; As Above, So Below; Door Is A Jar; Snapdragon;* and *Green Ink*

*Poetry*. She is a student at The Writer's Studio. Reading and writing poetry is how she stays alive and engaged with a turbulent world.

**Patty Somlo** has published four books, including *The First to Disappear* (Spuyten Duyvil), a finalist in the International Book Awards, Best Book Awards, and National Indie Excellence Awards; *Even When Trapped Behind Clouds: A Memoir of Quiet Grace* (WiDo Publishing), an honorable mention in the Reader Views Literary Awards; and *Hairway to Heaven Stories* (Cherry Castle Publishing).

**Robert Spiegel** is a writer living in Albuquerque. He works as a senior editor for *Design News*. His fiction, poetry, memoir, and drama have been published in such diverse publications as *Gargoyle, Fleas on the Dog, Rolling Stone*, and *True Confessions*.

**Anna Steegmann**, a native of Germany, is a bilingual writer based in New York City. She has been teaching writing at City College New York since 2005 and is a staff writer for *New York City Jazz Record*. Her essay "Mein Harlem (Epiphany)" was selected Notable Essay of 2007 for *The Best American Essays 2008*.

**Sidney Stevens** has an MA in journalism from the University of Michigan. Her short stories are forthcoming or have appeared in literary journals, including *Oyster River Pages, Woven Tale Press, Scribble, Hedge Apple, Wild Word, Bright Flash Literary Review, OyeDrum*, and *The Centifictionist*. Her creative nonfiction has been published in *Newsweek, The Dillydoun Review*, and *Nature's Healing Spirit*.

**Alison Stone** has published seven collections, including *Zombies at the Disco* (Jacar Press), *Caught in the Myth* (NYQ Books), and *They Sing at Midnight* (2003 Many Mountains Moving Poetry Award). Her work is in *The Paris Review, Poetry, Ploughshares*, and many others. She won *Poetry*'s Frederick Bock Prize and *New York Quarterly*'s Madeline Sadin Award. She created The Stone Tarot.

**Lou Storey** is a retired psychotherapist living in Savannah, GA with Steve, his husband of thirty-four years. Lou's fiction and creative nonfiction writings have appeared in *New Yorker, New York Times Tiny Love Stories, River Teeth's Beautiful Things, Beyond Queer Words Anthology* and in journals related to creativity, mental health, and issues connected to LGBTQ older adults.

**James Wyshynski** is a former editor of the *Black Warrior Review*. His poems have appeared in *American Poetry Review, Connecticut River Review, Hayden's Ferry Review, Nimrod, River Styx, Stoneboat, Terminus, Beloit Poetry Journal, Cincinnati Review, Cortland Review, Valum*, and others. His manuscript, *Emigrant from an Imagined Country,* is in search of publisher.

## Editors/Publishers

HEATHER TOSTESON is the author of seven books of fiction, poetry and non-fiction, most recently the novel *The Philosophical Transactions of Maria van Leeuwenhoek, Antoni's Dochter (1668-1696)* and a poetry collection *Source Notes: Seventh Decade*. She has an MFA (UNC-Greensboro) and PhD in English and Creative Writing (Ohio University). Her work in health communications focused on cross-disciplinary communication, racism, social trust, and how belief systems develop and change. Most recently, she and Charles Brockett co-authored *Sharing the Burden of Repair: Reentry After Mass Incarceration*, an extensive six-year Wising Up Listening Project. She has co-edited all eighteen Wising Up Anthologies.

CHARLES BROCKETT has a PhD from UNC-Chapel Hill and is a recipient of several Fulbright and National Endowment for the Humanities awards. A retired political science professor, he has written two well-received books on Central America, numerous social science journal articles and book chapters, and most recently the ebook *President Biden and the Prospects of Immigration Reform: A Wising Up Citizen Scholar Report*. With Heather Tosteson, he is co-founder of Universal Table and Wising Up Press and co-editor of the Wising Up Anthologies.

Visit our website and learn about our other publications,
our readers' guides, and calls for submissions.

www.universaltable.org
wisingup@universaltable.org

P.O. Box 2122
Decatur, GA 30031-2122

www.ingramcontent.com/pod-product-compliance
Lightning Source LLC
Chambersburg PA
CBHW030852170426
43193CB00009BA/580